Between Animal and Man:
The Key to the Kingdom

By Michael W. Fox

Integrative Development of Brain
and Behavior in the Dog
The Behavior of Wolves, Dogs
and Related Canids
Understanding Your Dog
Understanding Your Cat
Concepts in Ethology: Animal and Human Behavior
Between Animal and Man:
The Key to the Kingdom

Books for children by Michael W. Fox

The Wolf
Vixie, The Story of a Little Fox
Sundance Coyote
Ramu and Chennai:
Brothers of the Wild

Between Animal and Man

Dr. Michael W. Fox

D.Sc., Ph.D., B.Vet.Med., M.R.C.V.S.

Coward, McCann & Geoghegan, Inc.   New York

SBN: 698-10710-1

Library of Congress Cataloging in Publication Data

Fox, Michael W   1937-
  Between animal and man.

  Bibliography: p.
  1. Psychology, Comparative. I. Title.
BF671.F64   1976   179   76-4952

PRINTED IN THE UNITED STATES OF AMERICA

Contents

Author's Note

Foreword

1 The Emotions and Needs of Animals and Man 15

2 The Extra Sense of Man and Beast 29

3 The Rhythm of Life in Animal and Man 33

4 Love, Dependency, and Perpetual Infants 44

5 Animal and Human Displays: Skin, Fur, and Clothes..... 62

6 The Skin Trade: Wild Furs and Murder 84

7 Hunters and Humane Values 90

8 Man, Progress, and Ecology 104

9 Creation, Conservation, and the Future of Man 112

10 Some Issues and Actions in Conservation 116

11 Social and Psychological Aspects of Ecology 135

12 Animal and Human Awareness; Superiority and
    Racism 155

13 Levels of Consciousness: Animal and Man 169

14 The Three Stages of Man 175

15 The Other Side of Communication and Consciousness 182

16 From Amoeba to Man 188

17 The End of Dreams: Man Is Animal and God 203

Afterword 221

Suggestions for Further Reading 224

Acknowledgments

The author is especially grateful to Patricia Brehaut Soliman for her constructive editorial comments and for her encouragement in completing this work. And he wishes to thank Allan Garshman for his excellent copy-editing job. Thanks also to Herb Whitman and Stewart Halperin, whose fine photography adds greatly to my own photograph endeavours.

To all creatures great and small

Author's Note

This is a book about animals, people, reverence for life, conservation, and consciousness raising. When we see other animals, people, wilderness and all, not in terms of how they can fulfill our own needs and expectations, but in terms of their own intrinsic worth, and relate with all of life with reverence and ethical responsibility, then it will be a different world. The world is how we perceive and interact with it. If it is seen only as fulfilling human wants, and if we continue to extract, exploit, control, and manipulate it and one another alike, there will be no hope for the future, and our lives will continue to be shallow and empty.

"See me for what I am and not as you might use me" is the silent cry of wilderness, of wolf and whale; it is also the cry of many people today, women and men who are concerned about human potential and the future of their children. Wolf and Indian alike say, "Know yourself and know me as your brother—let us share this world for there is no other."

Reverence for all life may prevent man's inhumanity to both man and animal and his unremitting destruction of the natural world and its resources. Commitment to life may make us more responsible as stewards of this planet. Reverence alone without action is not enough; without really seeing and knowing ourselves, it is blind and dangerous faith.

In this book, through understanding something of the nature of animals and of our kinship with them, a sense of reverence and commitment may surface, and with it, I hope, the urgent realization that we alone are responsible for this earth and for the future of all creatures great and small.

Michael W. Fox

Foreword

It was during the terrible winter of 1947 that, as a child, I decided to become a veterinarian. At that time I had several lost and starving stray dogs to care for. Throughout my childhood my closest companions were dogs, and together we would explore and discover the wonders of the English countryside. That playground is now gone forever under a suburban housing development, but those early years with nature are still alive in my mind. When I graduated from veterinary college, I knew a lot about diseases and the healing arts, but nothing about normal behaviour or animal psychology. Over the past decade I have researched this field extensively, domestic dogs leading me to study wild canids—wolves, coyotes, and foxes—whose behaviour has been little altered by man (compared to the dog, whom man has almost made into his own image). My wolves then led me on an unexpected but necessary path, away from science and knowledge for knowledge's sake and into conservation and human values. Being wild and "pure", and different in many ways from domestic dogs, they also led me to study some of the consequences of domestication. After a time with Eskimo hunters in the Arctic and "primitive" forest gatherers in South India, my wolves brought me full circle to look at myself, a highly "civilized" being, in relation to these ancestral cultures of my own forefathers. Once we were all hunter-gatherers, and, in fact, only for a small fraction of evolutionary time have we had domesticated plants, animals, and technology.

So my interest in animals and nature flowed to embrace interest and concern for the nature of man and for man's relationship with nature. This book therefore reflects the development of my own interest and thinking. Understanding is the key to the kingdom, and my search for knowledge has helped open this door that is so often closed between animal and man. From objective scientific enquiry, kinship with animals and reverence for all life has emerged, together with a deeper understanding of myself and others. Unfortunately the "animal experience" is not the way for everyone, although we are all animals! Perhaps the truth lies in the observation of one great American Indian chief who, at the end of the last century, observed that the demise of the white man is that he sees the world as his, rather than seeing himself as a part of the world. And in our own culture Thoreau saw that in wilderness lies the preservation of the world. I believe that a person who is close to nature is close to understanding himself, and that man is both animal and god. Man has the emotions and the basic needs of an animal—there is nothing intrinsically wrong with human nature: It is nurture and culture that create so much chaos, alienation, and misunderstanding. Man is also god in terms of his potential awareness and responsibility to all living things.

Between Animal and Man addresses these issues and focuses specifically on man-animal relationships and similarities, as well as man's commitment to nature and to understanding himself. It will hopefully be for many a key to the kingdom and help foster what Albert Schweitzer urged—a reverence for all life. He observed that "An ethics that does not also consider our relation to the world of creatures is incomplete—by ethical conduct toward all creatures, we enter into a spiritual relationship with the universe."

We may also discover that between animal and man is a world of wonder and beauty which can be a part of our lives and which will enrich our lives with understanding and compassion.

Between Animal and Man:

The Key to the Kingdom

Courtship hug in canids—

—and similar expressions in man. It is our doing, not our being, that separates us from animals and from each other.

1

The Emotions and Needs of Animals and Man

I remember being outraged at overhearing a conversation between two men involved in animal research at a lunch given by a large pet food company. It was their view that the behaviour of animals is controlled by instinct (a concept which is emptily bandied about and personified like "mother nature"). Since instinct directs the lives of cats and dogs like some automatic pilot, its adherents imply, such animals obviously don't have to think very much. And, they conclude, being so simple compared to man, who has ideas, imagination, and can make things with his hands, animals must therefore be incapable of reason and of experiencing true emotions.

Such thinking stems from modern man's alienation from the animal kingdom. Alienated by an arrogant ego enamoured of its own technological and material prowess, alienated by a deeply ingrained religious philosophy that man is something unique, created differently from the rest of nature—man stands separate and apart in increasingly lonely isolation. In spite of the work of Charles Darwin and others who have established that we evolved from apes, it is generally accepted that our evolutionary progress since then has been so accelerated, taking us so far from our ani-

Subtle changes in facial expressions in an infant communicate mood and emotions ranging from surprise, to happiness, apprehension to displeasure.

Alert
alpha

Passive indifference

Alert and
"happy"

Friendly
grin
(ears up)

Open-mouth
play face

Friendly
submissive
face

Consummatory "pleasure" face
(eyes closed)

Submissive grin
(ears back)

Threat stare; Submissive Grin

Intense threat

Threat by
superior

Defensive gape

Various facial expressions in the wolf, many of which are similar to those of man.

mal ancestors, that man is indeed no longer *just* an animal. Animals therefore cannot have similar needs or experience comparable emotions to man.

In contrast to this view, some American Indian tribes have the same word for people and for animals, making no distinction between animal and man: *We are one and animals are our brothers and sisters.* This philosophy of acceptance and oneness is crucial today if animal conservation programs are to survive.

Imagine meeting a nomadic desert bushman. As you sit waiting for the mission translator to come and help you communicate, you look around his temporary village: All he and his fellow tribesmen have are a few brush piles to sleep under, perhaps a throwing or digging stick or hunting spear, and that's about all. In fact, it is all they need, except for the odd hand-fashioned musical instrument and an ostrich egg to carry water. So primitive in their technology, they seem little more than apes or Stone Age relics of modern man. At last the translator arrives, and he introduces you to a wizened old man who invites you to sit next to him in the dirt beneath the shade of a brush pile. You ask him how old he is and he replies, "I am as young as the most beautiful wish in my heart and as old as all the unfulfilled longings of my life."*

Suddenly you realize you are seated next to a man of knowledge—a man more in touch with the world around him and with himself than you are. I believe, too, that if we had the right translator, we might experience the same sense of humility and wonder at other fellow beings on this earth who have neither developed nor need any technology to lead a full life—the whales, the wolves, the dolphins.

Today's mechanistic education tends to destroy the natural sense of wonder and oneness most children feel for animals and nature. Science's reductionist (simplifying) approach to animals —often using them to test the effects of various drugs or other experimental procedure—prevents the student from seeing and appreciating the animal for itself. It is not regarded as a living, grow-

---

* From Carol and Marlin Perkins, *I Saw You from Afar*, Atheneum, 1965.

ing, and adapting being, but simply as tissue for experimentation. In fact, it is considered unscientific to attribute humanlike emotions to animals: This is what anthropomorphism means. Yet I believe that it is unscientific today *not* to consider such possibilities, and there is a growing body of evidence to support this.

But how about a fly or a tree? As soon as there is life within a single cell, there must be a rudimentary awakening of consciousness, and, with increasing complexity, there will be more consciousness, until a sense of self in relation to others begins to develop. To experience kinship with a fly or a tree is to accept the fact that we all come from the same source—that within our bodies there is something more than mere chemical affinity with all things of this earth, from which we have come and to which our bodies will return. In our bodies as well as in a fly is the wisdom of the earth. Such awareness can open our minds to the oneness of all things within all time and space. We may experience life as a continuously evolving and involving process of expression and impression; of expansion and unity; of contraction and individuation. Beyond life, as though life itself were a preparation for it, is the unitive ocean of pure consciousness, where nothing but the essence of our lives endures—where worldly possessions, needs, goals, and ideals are cast off. And in living, such a moment of eternity can be experienced when we are free to see a fly or a tree and, being unattached to our personal world, allow such things to take us out of ourselves.

But I am talking here about the experience—religious or mystical—when one of man's highest needs is fulfilled, whereas my task now is, rather, to explore the emotions and needs of our fellow animals. In talking about them we cannot separate either the influences of man upon them (since many of them are domesticated) or both their and our behaviour and emotions. We are both biologically related and also socially related, since many animals have lived together with man and have been influenced by him during more than ten thousand years of civilization and domestication. Because of our biological link with other animals, especially the carnivores and primates, I believe it is important for humane and conservation reasons that people know such

Many of the rituals and social patterns of animals are analogous to and serve the same function as those seen in man. Courting swans form lifelong bonds, and prairie dogs live cooperatively in village communities.

animals do indeed have many needs and emotions (feelings) which are like our own. An appreciation of this may make a hunter think twice about killing "just an animal," or a woman reject wearing furs of wild animals not "harvested" like fruit, but crushed instead like helpless children in steel traps. Such knowledge might also help people see that wild animals have rights as well as emotions and needs like us, and that therefore they have as much of a right to live as we do, even though our priorities and our immediate needs may dictate their destruction.

Few people realize that isolating a laboratory rat, dog, or rhesus monkey from its companion cage mates can be emotionally stressful, as well as influential to the significance of a researcher's experimental conclusions. Perhaps familiarity breeds contempt, or the researcher protects himself from his guilt at destroying animals in his work by turning them into test subjects, giving them numbers. A veterinarian or human doctor may also protect himself from failure—from the deep sense of hurt and inadequacy when a patient dies—by depersonalizing them. The cold, objective approach to the patient, who becomes a nonperson on a case history card, may also be a product of scientific rather than humanistic education: The disease is "a process"; the patient an amalgam of "symptoms". His needs and emotions are neglected, even though they may be the real key to a cure, rather than a scalpel or drugs.

Think, too, of our domesticated farm animals—cattle, sheep, pigs, and poultry—raised en masse on modern, fully automated factory farms. It is an efficient way to feed the world. But are such animals, raised like vegetables, being treated humanely? Hopefully from the farmer's viewpoint, their temperaments have been sufficiently altered through selective breeding so they may adapt to such conditions and *behave* like machines, efficiently and quietly converting cheap vegetable and fish protein into animal protein, or, in other words, adapt without undue stress. Otherwise, this food conversion process will finally prove less than efficient, and perhaps then, on economic rather than humane grounds, the farmer might be forced into becoming concerned. Perhaps with the knowledge that some of his animals still *have* feelings, he will attend more closely to their needs and uphold the tradition that a farmer cares more for his stock than for his pocket.

Certainly the need for affection and companionship are the animal needs that most closely resemble human needs. If the relationship with the loved one is threatened, sibling rivalry and jealousy may develop in animal and man alike. We see this when a child or a cat or dog is threatened by the advent of a new member of the family, be it a new baby, a kitten, or a puppy. Or if a close emotional bond is broken, as by hospitalization (separation from home and family), depression, refusal to eat, and increased susceptibility to disease are common results in cats, dogs, and human infants alike. All three have not only the same basic needs but also virtually the same centres in the brain where these emotions arise. Add to this the fact that the relationship between child and parent and pet and owner is often very similar. Then it is not surprising that changes in relationships should bring about similar emotional responses.

Now extrapolate this to wild animals—wolves, coyotes, bobcats, and mountain lions. They, too, have close emotional ties, especially between mates and between parent and offspring, and would be no less adversely affected by separation from their kin than any of us, or our cats and dogs.

In my book *Understanding Your Cat,* I emphasised that because cats are less dependent than dogs, they are less easily trained and also suffer fewer emotional problems. For example, it is difficult to instill a sense of guilt in a cat. Although it can be taught what it may or may not do in the house, it will rarely show obvious remorse when you come home several hours after it has done wrong. By contrast, you can always tell if a dog has done something he shouldn't have.

Such guilt in some of our pets certainly implies that they have a conscience and a sense of self and other (if not I and Thou) akin to our own. The average dog, well-socialized or bonded to its master, reveals other qualities often wished for in human relationships—loyalty, unconditional affection and acceptance, obedience and conscientiousness. Some dogs, bonded like this, have

Photo: S. Halperin

Adult chimps play indulgently with an infant, and an old male derives obvious pleasure from another.

been known to pine away and eventually die after the master's death. This closeness between man and dog is almost as unique in the animal kingdom as it is between man and man. It has been developed in the dog by thousands of years of domestication, making it open to being closely tied to its owner, who serves both as "parent and pack leader." This potential is realized by early socialization with man during a critical period in the pup's life. Without the right social experiences during this period, bonding will never develop. Exactly the same process operates in human infants, and experience with adoption shows there is a similar critical period for bonding. In fact, both dog and human go through almost identical stages of emotional development.

One of the highest human virtues is altruism—caring for others unconditionally with no thought of personal gain. Again this quality is not exclusive to human beings: Examples are to be seen throughout the animal kingdom. A herd of elephants will defend a sick companion and attempt to get it onto its feet; dolphins will likewise defend an injured companion and will hold it up above the water so it can breathe. Swimmers in distress have occasionally been rescued by dolphins. (Yet forty thousand or more of these beautiful mammals are killed each year in tuna nets and may soon be extinct, where with little extra cost those nets could be modified so that dolphins would not get caught up in them.) An injured wolf will be brought food by the rest of the pack. In our pets we see one house cat gently grooming a sick companion or its owner when he or she is feeling ill or depressed.

Cases of heroism in our canine companions also point to a higher awareness of self and others' needs, as dramatized in classic stories like that of the loyal dog that held its little master above the ice until the boy could be pulled out. Opponents of this point of view would explain many cases of so-called altruism more simplistically, claiming that the dramatic rescue of a family from fiery death by the dog or cat that awakens them is due solely to the coincidence of the animal's being excited by the smoke and flames. Quite different, though, is the case often reported in our newspapers of a pet actually going into a burning room to bring out a human companion.

NEED HIERARCHY

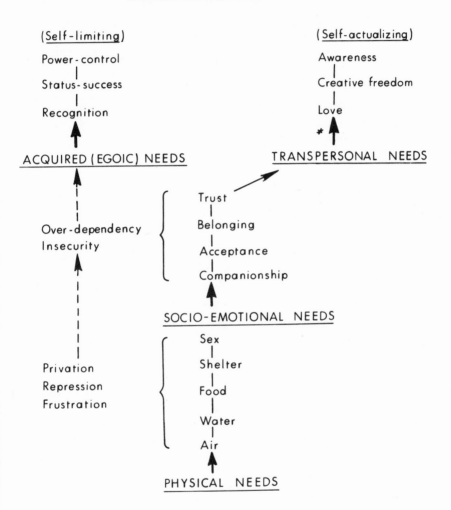

Lack of fulfillment of basic physical needs in humans leads to privation, repression, and frustration. Social and emotional needs, if not met, may give rise to insecurity, "identity crisis," and dependency. (The self-limiting egocentric needs, such as the need for power, may compensate for frustration of social and emotional needs.) Western society generally reinforces the egoic needs more than the transpersonal needs.

It may be concluded then that the evidence points to those animals closest to man in evolutionary history—the monkeys and apes, and also the carnivores, wolves, dogs, cats, and elephants, whales and dolphins sharing several emotions and needs similar, if not identical, to man. The need for companionship—to belong—and the subjective emotional experiences of pleasure, affection, jealousy, fear of rejection and depression associated with this need, are seen in all social animals. And the need to conform in order to be accepted and to forgo some degree of personal freedom and autonomy in satisfying one's personal wants, is manifested in all group-living animals: in the tribe of people, the pack of wolves, and the troop of monkeys. In these more sociable, conforming, and dependent animals altruism as well as guilt (conscience) can be observed. Each animal may be bound to the group through the strong ties and needs of affection and socialization as well as for reasons of its own survival. Because of these ties the animal cannot usually leave if there is tension in the group, and a dominant overlord may make the lives of subordinates thoroughly miserable. Status struggles for rank and power, oppression of weaker ones and paranoid responses to these dramas, seem to develop consistently in tightly structured animal and human societies alike. In modern man the need for recognition, success, status, power, financial wealth, and control over others stems from this. The more autonomous, nonconformist, strong willed and inner-directed people of such a system avoid *some* of its sicknesses; they are more catlike, if you wish, than the obedient, faithful and subservient underdogs.

There is a delicate balance between conformity and independence, autonomy and interdependence, and unconditional love and the bonds and obligations of kinship between self and others. This dilemma of conflicting need—to be free and to belong—must face every social animal living in a troop, pack, or tribe. The conflict is perhaps most intense in modern man, who is highly individuated but who has the social complexity and corporate anonymity of an ant!

Perhaps to be healthy today we must be both cat and dog. In

being flexible, in being more catlike or inner-directed, we may avoid many of the stresses and neuroses to which the sociable and dependent dog is prone. But we must not be *totally* inner-directed; otherwise we will forgo the social advantages of being gregarious and cooperative! Indeed the cardinal thing that *does* separate man from animals is his remarkable *flexibility* in assuming different roles appropriate to a wide range of contexts. This versatility, coupled with his unique ability to fabricate new contexts as well as to create artificial environments, makes him not only the most sophisticated tool user in the animal kingdom, but also enables him to create social tools. Indoctrination, mass programming with to produce goods and consumer needs to accommodate them, the appeal to idealism, the stirring up of political or religious fervor new technologies of communication, the creation of industries and militant enthusiasm—all these social tools produce further needs and conflicts, values and aspirations, and can make man, as a cultural being, victim of his very potential. They give him the freedom to control his own destiny and at the same time can be his downfall.

With the growing complexity of the individual brain and with the intrinsic complexity of society, there is increasing consciousness to a degree unprecedented in other life forms on earth. It is as though mankind, the fruit of the entire process of evolution, has come to contain within its essence the seeds of a universal awareness from which all life has evolved and to which man may return in consciousness. Thus evolution ultimately turns in on itself as an involution—as reflective consciousness.

Man therefore knows that he knows, but I believe an animal simply knows. Because of this, man is potentially both animal and god in terms of consciousness, but the irony is that today he is rarely either. "Animal" feelings and desires are often culturally oppressed or sublimated. Man gets caught in his own consciousness at the level of being able to "bind time"—to look ahead and to plan for the future. Caught up this way he becomes a goal- or achievement-oriented automaton no longer in touch with his body or with the world around him in the here and now. He becomes, then, something *less* than an animal—a pathetic robot striving to fulfill countless futile tasks and needs. With such tunnel vision awareness is constricted and the full potential of the human mind is never realized. And on such a "head trip" the body itself, instead of flourishing, becomes overspecialized and, like the mind, parts of it decay or become stiff and inflexible, while other parts may be so overdeveloped as to interfere with the functioning of the whole system.

Look at the bodies of animals and of "primitive" people who have not been subject to cultural programming. Consciousness is in the here and now, and the body is sensuous, lithe, and totally integrated with the mind. It was the philosopher Descartes who proposed a separation of mind from body. He was so deeply wrong, since they are parts of a unitive whole—yet coming from and observing his own culture, he was perhaps right! And he is perhaps still right today, but, as described in Chapter 17, what he thought to be normal for "modern" man is probably grossly abnormal.

Again, man's ability to bind time and to plan for the future is a tremendous asset, but, like culture itself, it may lead him to the fulfillment of all his potential or cripple and even destroy him. Couple these possible traps with inner- versus other-directedness (the conflict between a man's personal needs and values and those of the consensus of the culture in which he seeks acceptance and whose rejection he fears) and the "global neurosis" of mankind is easily understood. This complex of interacting forces is the final evolutionary step or corridor of fire through which man must pass in order to reach the eternal light beyond. What will man do, then, when all his needs are fulfilled? He will, indeed, be a very different creature, pure in consciousness and also in heart and being.

2

The Extra Sense of Man and Beast

A friend of mine, who spent several years studying animals, wild and tame, told me an intriguing story. In her apartment she had a cat and a dog accustomed to being left when she went out to work. One day, though, a distressed neighbor in the next apartment met her as she came home. That morning the two animals had been barking and meowing, making a tremendous racket, and the neighbor thought she heard someone talking to them. At about the same time that the animals became so excited, my friend learned later, her mother had died in a hospital. Had she "visited" the pets, which were very close to her, or was their behaviour just coincidence?

Similarly, my former wife's dog suddenly howled and showed obvious distress at about the moment when its aged companion dog was put to sleep at the veterinarian's. The dog hadn't known where its companion was going in the car that day, but like the cat and dog in the preceding anecdote, it obviously reacted to *something*. What did it in fact experience; what affected it and what, if anything, did the dog actually know?

A wolf malamute entered Madison Square Garden a few years ago with its second owner, not knowing beforehand that its former owner would be there. Suddenly, amid a crowd of thousands, the wolf dog was alerted; it howled and proceeded to cross the great hall without hesitation to greet its former master. In such a crowd the sense of smell could surely have played no part. Or could it? In attempting to account for apparently incredible animal feats, one must consider their basic, well-developed sensory abilities before concluding that some are simply inexplicable and involve some extrasensory ability. The remarkable cases of cats and dogs, lost in the country or on another side of the city, managing to find their way home cannot be explained on the basis of simple scent-trailing, since the animal often travelled away from home by car. Visual cues can often be ruled out, too, because the journey was made at night or the animal confined in a traveling cage and was unable to see outside. But there must still be a logical explanation. We know homing pigeons can use the sun as a compass; they have an exact sense of time, an inner sense of where the sun should be at their home at a given time of day. Displace the animal and the sun is in a slightly different position. Migratory birds can also use the stars to navigate by, and there is some evidence that geomagnetic influences from the earth play some role. Perhaps geomagnetism explains why my friend Roger Caras' dogs become so excited when they get near their weekend home outside New York City. No matter what route they take, or what time of day or night it is, the dogs know—even waking from deep sleep—when the car is close to home. Perhaps they pick something up from their master, or perhaps each place has its own characteristic geomagnetic qualities. In spite of blizzards, complete whiteouts in an unrelieved terrain with no obvious landmarks, an Arctic Eskimo can find his way home with little difficulty. It seems there is a sense of place and, possibly related to this, what we often refer to as a "spirit of place."

Saint Bernards employed to rescue people trapped under the snow have great difficulty finding a dead person, but not one who is still warm. The cue here is not likely to be smell, since a thick blanket of snow covers the body. Could it be psychic? Recent research reveals another explanation. Dogs possess infrared heat detectors in the nose; so it is a physical rather than psychic ability that enables the Saint Bernard to find a living person buried deep under an avalanche.

But solar navigation, geomagnetism, sense of place, or infrared sensors still cannot entirely account for "psi-trailing." There are really incredible, authenticated cases of a dog or cat finding its owners in a place where it has *never, ever been before.* The pet has usually been left with neighbors or relatives near its former home, and its owners have moved many miles—sometimes hundreds of miles—to a new home. What cues does the animal pick up to enable it to find its owners again?

There are many anecdotes by anthropologists who have seen bushmen "feel-see" things that, with our ordinary senses, we cannot detect. One may divine for water or know that a particular food plant or animal is just over the next hill. Is this simply coincidence, where something within and without coincide in space-time at a frequency higher than chance or random probability? If so, then Einstein's theory of relativity and the simple laws of cause and effect must be revised.

I believe there is more to these phenomena than our rational, logical minds can accept or analyze. In our everyday lives we often experience empathy with others, and when we are relaxed our insight and intuition can do more than the tunnel-vision, achievement-oriented, need-directed rational mind. When mind and body are relaxed and integrated with feeling, a higher state of sensitivity, of receptivity, may be experienced. The mind can "feel-see," using the whole body as a receiving and transmitting organ. How else can one explain psi-trailing in animals, homing in surely on the "vibrations" of their owners. The unitive force at the level of emotions is affection—that powerful universal bond of animals and man. How else can one explain a bushman's certainty as he points to the empty horizon and says he "feel-sees" a sick friend coming to his camp. The anthropologist sees and feels nothing, but a day later that very man comes into camp from the precise direction in which the "primitive" had pointed. There are accounts of Australian aborigines who can, if given a possession of the person to be followed, track him over a trail that is months old.

Philosophers and mystics have long alluded to a collective consciousness (the noösphere of Teilhard de Chardin) and the possibility, first proposed by Hermes, that the whole universe is originally and ultimately mental or psychic. Modern physics has shown us that what we perceive as "solid" matter is simply energy in varying degrees of density or concentration and frequency. We still have a long way to go before we understand what the transition point is between physical and psychic energy, between the unconscious "presence" of matter and the conscious presence of living things; with greater complexity of the structure (the brain) there is more consciousness, more psychic energy.

I am on my way home now on an earlier flight. I wonder if my family knows it since I am thinking about them. And who will be the least surprised to see me—the dog, the cats, my children, or my wife? There is much to learn from these amazing feats of animals and men. I wonder about animals and those people closer to a sense of the earth than we are. A man who knows, who can "feel-see," could probably not tell me how he does it. Perhaps our way of life and our technology are drawing us away from the need to use these extrasensory abilities which I believe are latent in us all. I also believe they are developed to some degree in animals and can be extremely well developed in some "primitive" peoples as they were once in us, before we became civilized and separated from the world and from each other. It is hoped this sixth integrative sense will be rekindled in us as we rediscover our kinship with all life and the true brotherhood of mankind.

3

The Rhythm of Life in Animal and Man

All animals, including man, have a distinct, cyclic pattern in much of their behaviour and body functions. Some of these are inborn, like the sleeping patterns of nocturnal and diurnal animals; the daily (circadian) rise and fall in our body metabolism and temperature and the monthly menses; the seasonal moults, migrations, and breeding periods in animals. These long and short cycles are all interwoven and are set with incredible precision by internal physiological "clocks." Some of these "clocks" are unaffected by external influences such as a change in day length or temperature, while others are more susceptible. These "soft clocks" can be reset after a while to respond to external influences, as when one experiences "jet lag" in travel from one side of the continent to the other. We now know that when one or more of these "clocks" is not set properly, the disruption can be extremely stressful to the body. Rest seems crucial after disruption of body time to allow that part of the body to reset itself, since it is more vulnerable to infection and possibly to psychosomatic stress reactions at such times.

It is principally because of these clocks that animals in the wild seem to have such fixed and predictable habits for waking, grazing, hunting, drinking, playing, and so on. For obvious reasons, the cycles of hunter and hunted are often closely attuned. Similarly our pets attune their natural rhythms to ours, and in turn, our inborn rhythms are influenced by our culture and life-style.

We divide our days into periods—minutes, hours—a time to eat and a time to sleep, a time to work and a time to relax. These are all part of a great variety of rhythms man has "built in" to his own system or which he has imposed culturally upon himself.

There are also various subtle *internal* rhythms of the body—of its organs and cells. In man the white cells in the blood are minimal in number between twelve and six P.M., while they reach a peak from two to six A.M. There is also a daily periodicity in circulating hormones from the adrenal glands. These reach a peak between four and six in the morning, as a rule, and then drop off for the rest of the day. Apparently penicillin has its best effect when given in the late afternoon, and we all know that children are more likely to develop a fever in the early evening because the body temperature tends to increase normally at that time. Tied in with the biological body rhythms is our susceptibility or resistance to disease. In mice there is a greater resistance to certain toxins if they are administered at night. The death rate may differ by as much as seventy-five percent from the rate of those given the same toxin during the day. Therefore the time of day in which one is infected may well determine life or death.

The behaviour of the grunion fish of California provides a dramatic example of how external stimuli affect reproductive rhythms. The female deposits eggs in the shore sand only at the highest waters of each tide, and only with the highest tides of each month. Milt from the males runs through the sand and down the sides of the spawning females. The next wave returns the fish to the ocean. Eggs hatch two weeks later in synchrony with the next high tide. During the season, the female will make four to eight spawning runs. In this way lunar sub-cycles are imposed on an annual breeding season. Similarly sunlight has the effect of switching on sexual behaviour in birds, while in sheep it is a decrease in sunlight in the fall of the year that triggers it. Thus there are internal mechanisms that have, through the slow process of evolution, become tuned to external influences, like the phases of the moon or the passage of the seasons.

A number of diseases that are transmitted by insects show an interesting circadian rhythm. Malaria in man is one example, where the filaria in the bloodstream increase in number during the early evening. This coincides with the time when the mosquitoes are out and more likely to bite a person, and so pick up the infective organisms and deliver them to another host. It is remarkable how the internal parasite has attuned itself to the activities of the external mosquitoes, but we should not be surprised at these remarkably evolved timing patterns in animals. Similar "clocks" operate in the homing and migratory navigation of birds. It makes our acceptance, perhaps, of some of the claims of astrologers of lunar and solar influences seem not too far out. But science still has a long way to go before we can link physics and metaphysics!

Some body rhythms present in the newborn baby may be acquired from its mother. Here we face the astrological possibility that at the time of conception the fertilized egg is exposed to certain outside influences that affect the mother, and which in turn affect the fertilized egg. And so as the egg develops into an embryo, the timing of these external events, astrologists contend, could affect the development and timing of rhythmic activities in the embryo. Second, we must consider the time of birth, too—the season, the month, the position of the stars, and so on—which brings in the importance of astrology in determining "natal maps." Astrologers have maintained for decades that it is possible, by a knowledge of a man's or a woman's exact time and place of birth, to map certain astrological coordinates, and to construct what they call a "natal map," which purportedly reveals a great deal about the person's personality and his or her potential and weaknesses. Their assumption is that human beings are influenced by larger rhythms of activity—by the pulsing, ever-shifting changes in energy relationships between the stars and the planets.

A number of psychiatrists have found that mental patients have cyclic regressions. For example, the manic-depressive will have severe attacks, perhaps on a two- or three-month rhythm. And recently it has been shown that there is a high admission rate of patients into mental hospitals around the time of the full moon, a statistic reminiscent of the old folktales of moon-madness and werewolves.

Primitive man, out in nature, living in nature, was a part of the natural rhythms of the seasons and, being part of this continuum, he was perhaps better adapted than modern man. Ours is now less of a rhythmic kind of environment than one that affords a constant bombardment of stimuli with little respite. Yet modern man is at the same time insulated. In his centrally heated, air-conditioned home and automobile, with his manufactured clothing, he is less and less affected by the natural rhythms of the seasons. Also, the food he eats can be imported fresh or frozen and out-of-season from great distance. It can be stored so that his diet no longer reflects seasonal availability of foods, except in economically depressed areas. With artificial lighting he can drastically increase the length of daylight, and it has been shown in many animals that light has a very important effect on sexual behaviour and reproductive performance. So if modern man is being removed (or is removing himself) more and more from these natural, extraneous environmental rhythms, it must have some effect on his own internal rhythms—the rhythms of his body, his physiological functions; and of his mind, his psychological functions.

A change in the daily amount of exposure to artificial light in the house can influence the reproductive cycle of cats. Artificial lighting, heating and air conditioning seem to break the normal moulting pattern of cats and dogs so that they shed at odd times or almost constantly. It has been shown in laboratory mice that their longevity and their reproductive performance is enhanced by giving them an alternate diet of rich food and then less nutritious food every week or so. Perhaps the body *does* need varied stimulation as well as rest. It should not be overswaddled, because some stress itself can be beneficial. It is perhaps good to go hungry, to fast—to occasionally get those fat stores mobilized, instead of just maintaining oneself in a constant, hermetically sealed environment with all food provided and all bodily stresses minimized. This is certainly happening to modern man and to his pets, too, since they share the same environment.

While insulating us from nature's rhythms, modern life demands
that we be out front, up front, go, go, go all the time, and this
is increasingly stressful not only to the body but to the mind as
well. Modern man has to relearn *how to listen* to his body. He
may push himself unduly when he feels tired; in factories this
certainly ups productivity, but it also causes an up in accident
rates. We must listen to the body when we are working overtime.
We must listen to the body when we are on a definite work shift.
We must allow the body time to readjust to an altered work
schedule. We must listen to our bodies when we go abroad and
allow ourselves to reset our internal clocks to the local time before
we engage in a strenuous vacation or in intense business nego-
tiations.

We know now that there are indeed "morning" people and
"night" people. The morning people are those who, as soon as
they wake up, are alert and able to get on very efficiently with
their affairs. These people have been shown to have a high level of
circulating hormones from the adrenal glands first thing in the
morning. However, the night people and those intermediate people who reach their peak of activity later in the day have a very
low level of these circulating hormones when they first wake up,
and only as the day progresses do they build up. Thus there *are*
differences in the activity levels of people—those who are switched
on automatically on waking and those who need a longer time to
warm up. Consider a morning person and a night person going
to work, arriving at nine A.M. Which one will be more productive? There might be little difference, especially if the night person compensates—drinks gallons of coffee, smokes a lot of cig-
arettes to get himself up there. But ultimately, isn't he more likely
to succumb to one or another form of psychosomatic stress disease
—gastric ulcers or high blood pressure—than his inphase synchronized companion?

Society is large and complex enough now to be able to reor-
ganize to provide sufficient flexibility to allow people to work,
sleep, and seek recreation when they want to, in accordance with
their own natural rhythms, and not when they are "supposed" to.

Man has to relearn his own body, his natural rhythms, and go with the ebb and flow of life, not with the intense, continuous flow forced upon him by his culture that makes him an externally organized rather than an internally organized individual.* This is the ebb and flow that is more a part of nature, that is linked with astrological time, and that seeks its own cosmic order. The externally organized man falls out of phase with his own natural rhythms when forced by his culture to adopt *its* rhythm; increasingly he loses touch and also falls out of phase with the great cosmic rhythm of which he is a part.

This natural rhythmicity also influences the way we relate to each other. I tend to be a "double peak" person, having a peak of energy around midmorning and another in the early evening. I find it difficult to maintain a day-to-day relationship with a person who is an early morning person, or who only starts waking up late at night. If I try to alter my own natural rhythms to get in phase with that person, I find it very unsatisfactory, sometimes exhausting. Not that adaptation is to be avoided, for our systems *are* flexible, but even so we should seriously consider the problem of interpersonal desynchrony of rhythms. Of course the astrologers already have an answer to this which they derive from their natal charts—the "ideal" relationships with a synchronous sign. Nonetheless, we have a physiological and psychological problem in interpersonal relationships where people do have different rhythms, and the better we understand and listen to our own rhythms, the more sensitive we can be to the rhythms of others as well, so that we can maintain our relationships with them (especially intuiting their and our own mood shifts) with greater empathy and understanding.

There is evidence that all of us have distinct two- to three-week rhythms in each of three energy level systems†—intellectual, physical and emotional. Each energy level has its own particular rhythm, so that one week I might be very energized intel-

---

* One of the most effective ways of reestablishing rhythm is through relaxation-breathing as practiced in hatha-yoga and various forms of meditation. Prana (rhythmic breathing) can be the key not only to health, but to awareness of the harmony and unity of all things—the oceanic oneness of samadhi.

† See George Thommen, *Is This Your Day? Biorhythm Helps You Determine Your Life Cycles,* Crown, 1973.

lectually. Physically I might be quite low. However, I can manage because my head is in good shape. Another time I might be in a neutral phase emotionally. Then, the following week my intellectual and emotional energies might be very low, and this could lead to a brief day or two of depression until my physical and intellectual energies build up again. Quite possibly when these three energy levels reach a low point simultaneously, and when external pressures such as pressures of work are intense, their unfortunate conjunction could lead to a severe emotional breakdown, especially if the external stress continued for a few days and, with it, feelings of helplessness and no escape. This reminds us again of the cyclic patterns described by many psychiatrists in mental patients.

When he has to maintain a high and constant state of productivity a person is in a predicament. He must always be on the go, often in discord with his natural rhythms. Eventually, in order to modify his own rhythms sufficiently to fit into the unrhythmic, constantly high-pressured external situation he is involved in, he has to switch himself on with stimulants—and off with sedatives.

In trying to maintain this noncyclic activity pattern some people are running headlong toward a nervous breakdown (a general term for complete exhaustion of all three energy levels). Human beings and other animals, too, are like flowers, each having a time to close and a time to open; closing—withdrawal—is a time for reflection, rest, and recuperation. Opening is a time for experiencing, acting, encountering. The person who does not attend to these basic needs linked to his own rhythms will be doing a disservice both to body and to mind. A dramatic illustration of the sickness of this go-go-go kind of existence is the agitation and obvious distress in a group of city people waiting in a line in a grocery store or in the subway. They frequently seem unable to tolerate any kind of delay.

Years ago Pavlov was engaged in research with dogs of various personalities (or, to use his term, nervous typologies) and found that one type had a very excitable nervous system—if you like, a go-go dog—and could not tolerate enforced inhibition or any delay in reward. This dog was extremely likely to be beset by what Pavlov termed a neurosis. Its behaviour became disorganized, sometimes extremely aggressive, and there is a similarity here between Pavlov's dog of the excitable type and the person who has altered his nature to adapt to the high-stress, modern way of life, where everything is on the surface, where he has to keep up with the pace of things. Constantly on the go, he expects immediate reward, immediate gratification, immediate service, and, conversely, he becomes less capable of coping with delay and enforced inhibition and is easily frustrated, easily triggered to aggress.

Fritz Perls, the Gestalt therapist, recognized cyclic rhythms, notably of the ego boundary, and that people have their own natural rhythms of personality opening and closing, just like a flower. In the withdrawal phase a person turns inward to assimilate things, to repair, to recuperate, and then the next part of the cycle follows—a period of expansion, approach, engagement. The neurotic or anxious patient might not be able to tolerate excessive excitement which (as an arousal state) disturbs the normal rhythmic activities of mind and body. Tension, anxiety, insomnia, and even thyroid trouble can follow because there is some emotional stress upsetting the normal biological rhythms. Perls regards contact and withdrawal as the basic rhythm of life —the "pulsating persona." He sees a pathological state of withdrawal in the schizophrenic and in the psychotic, while a disorder involving extreme contact is seen in the overdependent person. These two patterns—complete withdrawal and overdependency— are good examples of a person's becoming fixed in one phase, either of openness or closedness, instead of maintaining the normal rhythm of the entire mind-body complex. Jung speaks of "diastole," or expansion, as extroversion of the libido, spreading to the entire universe, while "systole" is contraction into the individual. According to Goethe, to remain fixed in either of these attitudes means death.

Perhaps pathological extroversion—being out front all the time—is the most common disorder of our culture, and, indeed, is now considered normal. We have considered the possibility that when systems within the body fall out of synchrony, or when individuals fall out of synchrony with the external physical world or with each other, we have desynchronization and the possibility of some kind of psychological, physical or psychosomatic stress developing. I have referred to the ebb and flow of life and its psychic energy, and we can trace the possible link here in the individual from the time of conception, from life in the womb where the fetus develops its own rhythms . . . which are affected by the mother's rhythms . . . which in turn are affected by those of the outside world. Then we have the moment of birth, and the development of rhythms increasingly independent of the mother.

How much do the mother's activity rhythms influence the child *after* birth? Does she feed him, for example, on demand, or does she set up her own feeding schedule, and impose this on the developing infant? It is possible that a child raised in an environment that controls all his needs (the kind of world suggested by reading B. F. Skinner's *Beyond Freedom and Dignity*), becomes shaped by and dependent on such external forces. He grows up and is easily disciplined, easily molded; he is easily controlled because he is not autonomous and still seeks external support and direction. A child allowed to develop his own natural rhythmicity —in essence his individuality—will mature into a more complete (individuated) human being than one whose rhythms have been constantly interfered with and modified by others (who, in other words, becomes other-directed rather than self- or inner-directed). In fact, one strong point in favor of the open school system is to give the child freedom to learn when he wants to be active, when he wants to use his whole body, and at other times to withdraw into a corner quietly and read a book, or even to go to sleep, while other children on a different rhythm do something altogether different. The more we institutionalize—the more people we put together in the same school, the same hospital the same factory, the same office—the more we seem to make a general consensus and fix some arbitrary rhythm on the entire group that might well be stressful to those within it who have difficulty adapting.

According to Dr. Kurt Richter from the Johns Hopkins Medical School, man does not normally show as clear-cut a twenty-four-hour rhythm in such things as activity or body chemistry and metabolism as do apes or rats. He reports that monkeys and apes reveal sharp changes in activity and inactivity at twenty-four-hour intervals with great regularity in relation to light and darkness of the day and night, and that this had made many workers in the field conclude man must likewise manifest this clock. However, Richter points out that these workers overlooked one important difference between higher apes and man, and that is that for over 350,000 years since man's discovery of fire, he has had light from his hearth fire throughout the night, and so has no longer been exposed to alternating changes of light and total darkness. Richter proposes that man's survival has depended on his freeing himself from this twenty-four-hour timing device that produced such sharp changes in activity and behavior with relation to light and darkness. During the 350,000 years man has almost continually lived under conditions of constant light that required an even performance throughout most of the twenty-four hours. Now here we have something very significant to consider: As man develops a technology to control his environment we find that many of his normal biorhythms begin to disappear, or at least are less obvious than they are in monkeys and other animals. (Man does show diurnal or day-night changes in such functions as body temperature, pulse rate, and so on; but these changes are relatively slight.)

Under conditions of severe emotional shock or brain injury, however, Richter found that the natural biological rhythms may reappear. While it is clear that our culture, our way of life, affects many of our biorhythms, the reappearance of clear rhythmic activity in his patients can be interpreted another way. In their sickness they withdraw from reality and from the way of life that influences their rhythms; withdrawal (implosion) and regression to a more infantile or primitive rhythmicity may simply be part of the normal restorative healing processes of withdrawal. Psychotherapy might well concern itself more with restoring normal rhythmic functions in "stuck" patients who are always up (manic) or depressed (down), and here drugs can be of immense value in reactivating the cycle and literally getting patients "unstuck."

In conclusion, the mind and body of man and beast are governed by natural rhythms that have evolved in adaptation to the environment. Disturbances in them can lead to considerable physical and psychological stress. It is important with animals, therefore, to avoid disrupting their routine, since they are more creatures of habit and less flexible than (most) human beings. A break in routine can cause a drop in milk or egg production in cattle and poultry, and can lead to overexcitement and disruption of eating behaviour in dogs. An off-schedule run in the park after a habitually large evening meal can kill a dog from bloat or gastric torsion.

But overregimentation of daily activities can be mind-destroying, too, and is part of the "institutionalization" syndrome of mental patient and kennel dog alike. An occasional break in the *taedium vitae* is good for everyone. Some kennel managers avoid feeding their dogs on schedule and contend that the varied regimen keeps the dogs alert, more active, and healthy. This might be of great value for the mental health of zoo animals that have nothing to do between regular feeding times and that consequently fill the 'void' with a number of abnormal stereotyped behaviours, including pacing, rocking, and excessive grooming.

We must hear the lesson of nature in the rhythms of oceans and seasons and of trees and animals. To go with the ebb and flow, rise and fall, of all things within us and around us and also between us—as between man and man, and man and animal—is to be alive and living. This rhythm in all things—from the slow cadence of the cosmos to the shorter tempo of our lives and the brief moment of each cell in our body—is the complex pulse of life across the space-time continuum of eternity. Within the individuality of our own rhythms we are part of this greater whole and any man, cell, world, or animal that breaks away and loses its rhythmicity is dead or dying. The lesson, then, from nature is to go with the flow, with one's natural rhythms, and not push the river.

4

Love, Dependency, and Perpetual Infants

When we look at a mature, contemporary fellow human being and compare him with his nearest ape ancestors, the chimpanzee, the gorilla, and perhaps the orangutan, man looks like an infant. He has very little hair, the frontal ridge over his eyes is poorly developed, his beard is shaved, his skin is soft, he is not excessively muscular, he doesn't have enormous shoulders, or large teeth to display his dominance. We find, too, that many animals man has domesticated, like the pig and the cow, no longer resemble their wild counterparts; their hair is finer, their skin softer and thinner. Secondary features related to sexual maturity, like large horns and very thick skin over the shoulders, are also less developed. This phenomenon of underdevelopment of adult characteristics is called "neoteny" or "paedomorphosis." In domesticated animals it means they never really reach the full maturity of their wild ancestors, and that they do not expend energy, and therefore the food we give them, on developing these characteristics. Instead, they develop more flesh than bone, and consequently are more efficient food converters; neoteny in farm animals has great economic value.

But what if any, are the values of being relatively infantile for man? Again, such a question related to human behaviour can be illuminated by studying other animals. We find that in

Infantlike mouth licking by subordinate followed by leader seizing its muzzle in ritualized display of rank.

Subordinate bows to leader and then rolls over submissively.

Ritualized aggression in the wolf, low-ranking wolf bows and grins submissively to pack leader and is gently but firmly pinned to the ground. This is a display of dominance and serves to affirm the dominance/affection bond.

adult wolves there is much infantile behaviour—whining, crawl-
ing on the belly, urinating and assuming certain postures and
displays toward dominant adults, behaving toward the leader in
a way similar to cub toward parent. These are called "socio-
infantile" behaviours and they are important since they tend to
"cut off" (or defuse) aggression, to appease the aggressor and so
reduce conflict within the group. In certain species of birds we
find similar behaviour. During the breeding season the female
will stop the male aggressing when she is in his territory by
assuming an infantile food-soliciting posture. This remotivates the
territorially aggressive male, and he may then even feed her as
part of the courtship ritual. This behavioral or social neoteny—
the persistence or reappearance of infantile behaviours in adulthood—is also seen in many primates, such as chimpanzees and
rhesus monkeys, and also in man. We are all familiar with an
individual who in certain stress situations starts whining and
appearing submissive and obsequious. Psychiatrists might call
this regressive behaviour to a more infantile mode of expression
all in the service of the ego. Such behaviour in many animals,
including man, is of great social import in that it reduces conflict between individuals.

Cultural differences in the degree of acceptance and reinforcement of infantile behaviours should also be considered. To pub-
licly express feelings or emotions may be regarded culturally as
unmanly or immature. To adopt a certain immature mannerism
during particular social interactions, as when a subordinate encounters a superior may be a cultural norm. Here the regression
to a socially acceptable and socially expected infantile mode of
behaviour may be altogether normal, and illustrates the importance of looking at role playing, expectations, and "situational
personalities" in studying human behaviour.

We do many things to enhance our neoteny. One is to remove
the beard. The beard, in adult man, is potentially an aggressive,
sex and status-related signal. The use of deodorants, too, reduces
an important signal of one's individuality and rank (excuse the
pun). Of course, in medieval times and in some societies still,
men grew their beards, wore codpieces or gourds over their

genitals, padded their shoulders enormously, even padded their calves and wore headdresses to enhance their stature and display social status. But in modern Western society it is important to minimize conflict and so de-emphasize overt mature status, witness the relatively drab, clean-shaven, gray flannel-suited, deodorized urban businessman we see in the large anonymous herds. They suggest various species of birds that display bright plumage in the breeding season when they fight a lot and live apart, but moult and have drab feathers when they must live together in the winter. Similarly, deer shed their antlers and live peaceably after the breeding season.

In some societies, as in the wolf pack, social organization may involve leadership and the presence of an "alpha" or dominant individual. An alpha may be the only group member that does not have to display infantile behaviour, and he may assume and display full sexuality and rank and not have to wear low status gear or behave obsequiously. He can sport a large, bright headdress, enormous epaulets, or the largest gourd over his genitals. In the dominant male mandrill, a species of monkey, the alpha male has the brightest blue-red face (the same color as his genitals), while subordinate males have paler faces. The tribal or clan leader similarly may be the only individual to display status symbols—a crown, a sceptre, or the largest spear. Here we get into phallic symbolism in the leader who, by virtue of his status, is freed from the social pressures operating within the group where infantilism is important for group cohesion.

This could be interpreted, of course, as a kind of phallic domination, as it is by Reich, Roheim, Marcuse, and Freud. It is not difficult to take this line of thinking to the point Freud did, where leadership implies freedom to express or display full sexual maturity, while subordination under the phallus of the dictator involves repression of mature sexual and aggressive behaviours with inevitable psychiatric ramifications. However, if all individuals were aggressive, displaying their phallic symbols, there would surely be a reduction in social cohesiveness and cooperation. The "castrating" effect of social neoteny is clearly an extremely valuable attribute that facilitates group solidarity. There-

Response to a leader—wolves encircle the pack leader in a group display of allegiance, analogous to . . . the attentive circle of the football pack around their coach-leader.
Photo: Herb Whitman

fore, we can say that it may be important for groups to have a phallic leader or alpha individual, and for the majority to maintain infantile behaviours (although, of course, they are not infertile). The negative attributes of perpetuated infantilism may be more serious than phallic domination because individuals are more easily manipulated and controlled if they are repressed at a more infantile stage of ego functioning, and may be overdependent on each other and on the leaders who control their existence. In a true democracy such phallic leaders may be regarded as anachronisms, yet they emerge and are often revered by thousands of subordinate followers. It is a fact that most governments today would continue to function well (perhaps even better) without kings or presidents, although these symbolic figures may still play an important role in uniting the "masses."

The modern swing toward self-expressive, sometimes flamboyant clothes, the growing out of hair and beard, all are reactions against the conformity and anonymity of social neoteny. This resurgence of display is not necessarily related any longer to aggression, but is an indication of the individual's need to surface with a visible identity above the anonymous society that enfolds him.

This general phenomenon of neoteny, or paedomorphosis, also influences our choice of sex partners. Recently I did a study, using drawings of human male and female faces, in which one feature—nose shape, curvature of forehead, length or thickness of neck, or of the nose—varied, and we looked at preferences in male and female subjects. The study revealed that the most sexually attractive features of the male model were a fairly long nose, a thick neck and a medium forehead, while in the female more infantile characteristics, like a short, pert nose, slightly thick lips, large pupils, a large, curved forehead and thin, long neck were sexually attractive. We have good evidence that in the evolution of the human female there has been a strong sexual selection for infantile features (hence the term "baby doll"). There has also been an increase not only in sex-related neoteny, but in infantile characteristics related to social and aggressive contexts, where similar immature features are also seen in males, possibly to reduce conflict and aggression (e.g., removal of beard, tailored crotch to de-emphasize the presence of the genitals, etc.).* This is not only seen in the structure of the male but, as emphasized earlier, is also evident in the clothes that he wears.

With senility in many animals there is a loss of status and sex-related characteristics. We have balding of the hair, graying, loss of teeth, and shrinking of the body, and the aged individual might also return full cycle to infantile behaviour. This behaviour may release care-giving actions from others and may therefore ensure the survival of the senile members of the group. The same holds true for the infant. Its soft skin, its rounded features, are totally nonthreatening. Beating up a child or an old man is considered beyond the pale.† This is also true in many animals, where not only the behaviour, but also the colour and size of the infant inhibit aggressive males from attacking or even threatening. The young herring gull has brown feathers and is not attacked at shared feeding spots by white-feathered adults until it starts to moult; just as soon as the white feathers of the mature adult begin to appear, however, it will be attacked! In birds, too, we find a seasonal kind of infantilism, or at least a seasonal loss in sexual feathers, and regression to a more immature form; as mentioned earlier, many birds lose their courtship plumage so that during the winter they can form large flocks, perhaps for migrating. This loss of sexual and aggressive display signals reduces conflict and, again, helps the birds make up a large, anonymous group, like the men in their gray flannel suits!

There is a relationship between increasing infantilism and increased sociability. We find this true in the evolution of the canids. The more social canids like the wolves and African Cape hunting dogs show more infantile behaviour toward each other as adults than do, say coyotes and red foxes. Similarly cats show

---

* Although today some tailors are reemphasizing the crotch area again.

† Although child beating, quite common in this culture today, may be due to a breakdown in such aggression-inhibiting factors or to the child's need for independence conflicting with the parent's ego, since the battered-child syndrome is most common in children between three and five years old, the age when the infant ego begins to individuate from the earlier close "symbiosis" with the parent.

Mother wolf carries food to a cub (A & B) but disciplines one of her older yearling cubs (C & D) who also tries to solicit food. Overdependence is rare in wild animals since independence is essential for survival.

little infantile behaviour in adulthood and, compared to the dog, domestic cats are generally less neotenized, more independent and therefore less prone to emotional and behavioral disorders.

Our various breeds of domesticated dog are perhaps the best examples of neoteny, both in terms of structure—being much smaller, having smaller teeth, weaker jaws, and so on, than the wolf—and in terms of their behaviour. Many breeds are far more dependent than their wild counterparts, dependent in the sense that they will cry more when left alone. And they display more care-soliciting behaviour to their owners. This is partly attributable to an inherited disposition to behave in this way, and also to the way they have been raised. If they have been overindulged and made to feel dependent, they will be even more dependent than they intrinsically are. This can reach a pathological state. Of course, having such an overattached animal as a companion may fulfill many of its owner's needs, but it can lead to the variety of problems I have described in a recent book, *Understanding Your Dog.* Such pathologically neotenized dogs will develop a whole range of emotional disorders when their relationship with the owner is threatened, as it is by the birth of a child, by the introduction of a new pet, or by separation for some reason from the owners— the "perpetual puppy syndrome." Naturally there are advantages to having a dog which is somewhat dependent. This makes it easier to train and easier initially to socialize, but when over-dependency develops, it can lead to severe behaviour disturbance. We see exactly the same problem in man. The relationship between parent and child is often like the one between pet and owner, and there are many examples of both dogs and children developing similar psychological disorders like epilepsy, paralysis, asthma, and severe diarrhea.

Adult man, too, can have problems because of his susceptibility to pathological neotenization or, in other words, to becoming overdependent. Fritz Perls defines maturity as the state attained by the individual who can maintain himself independent of external support. An immature person is dependent on external emotional support. In man we find immaturity of ego when the person is fixated at one stage of personality development—

the fixation being reinforced or rewarded from without. Gestalt and other therapies teach how to function independently of such support, contending that maturity is, in essence, the attainment of independent, nonsymbiotic functioning based on the development of internal support. Children have many needs, and these are taken care of by their parents. But the parents are responsible for teaching the child to be increasingly independent, and there is a clear distinction to be made between love and dependency. However, in most relationships dependency exists in addition to love and can cause dangerous confusion.

Ideally a child matures to become independent, but very few do reach full maturity. They are never weaned from reliance on their parents, as society perpetuates a pathological neoteny or infantilism. The culture supports the child at school, then on to college, and when a person works for a company, "the company will take care of" many of his needs—and for the unemployed, the helping hands of the welfare state. This has great political significance. With a population of dependent, relatively immature adults, control and manipulation is more easily effected. This is a very different point of view from that of Freud, Marcuse, and Roheim, who propose that political control can be gained by repressing the sexual energy. This process of perpetuated dependency and of retarding maturation through a person's entire life span is something more than sexual repression—it is arresting growth!

In certain cultures the society even takes over the role of the mother, and the individual becomes totally dependent on the supportive social system, becoming in effect, socially overdependent. This is probably true of some communist countries, where children are taken at an early age into institutions and daycare centers. As adults they will be more easily molded and more compliant with the needs of the state, which is even referred to as the "mother" state. This is a good example of pathological infantilism in which the individual is *never* properly weaned, never capable of responsible autonomous functioning. The dependency needs are transferred from the natural mother to the society and, such needs are often transferred to the sexual partner

Photo: S. Halperin

As a mother chimpanzee slowly dies of old age, her mature son, abnormally overdependent, tries to solicit her attention. He spent several days beside her dead body, was depressed, did not eat, and soon after, died.

as well, who, having similar needs, is a partner in an immature relationship of mutual dependency rather than of mutual support and enrichment.

This dependency and infantilism has ramifications for relationships between lovers and friends alike. Consider two individuals who are not fully mature, with one form or another of dependency hang-up; a care-dependency relationship may be established that is often confused with love. One is dependent on the other and gives care to the other for fear of being rejected. This fear causes the recipient to increase his concern for the giver from a very selfish point of view. A sickening cycle of care-dependency, overdependency, and fear of rejection is perpetuated because this relationship is transferred from parents to children, and the children are molded in a society that rewards or reinforces it even further. It is essentially a fossilizing kind of infantilism: Emotional maturity and individuation are drastically arrested.

Dependency often underlies feelings of insecurity, of lack of trust, and of fear of rejection. This common human weakness is a cause of many severe emotional disturbances and is one of the main reasons for the breakdown of marriages and families alike.

Some would say I come down too hard on the dog in claiming that man made dog in his own image. They are probably right, since it is easy to underestimate the potential of most dogs when we see them in the home; the same dog could well fend for itself and revert to the wild as have many abandoned "feral" dogs, in spite of ten thousand years of domestication and a degree of dependency on its owner implanted in early life. I have drawn negative conclusions from the overdependency dogs display toward their masters, since it can be the cause of severe emotional disorders in dog and man alike. But, as with people, it is often easy to mistake dependency for closeness and conditional love for unconditional acceptance and affection.

It might be more fair to make the zoomorphic conclusion that dogs reflect the worst and best traits of mankind. The dog, in our everyday lives, not only is a mirror of our own nature but can also be the embodiment of humanity's highest qualities—acceptance, forgiveness, loyalty, truthfulness and openness, devotion, and unquestioning, unconditional love. This is why many prefer the company of animals, especially dogs, to people. Man had no hand in endowing the dog with such traits, although domestication and socialization help ensure his dog will display such behaviour toward him. Anyone seeing a family of wolves, the dog's "pure" cousin uncontaminated by human interference, will see the same traits. The lesson of nature is simple: Although the dog is man's best friend, could it be that man will someday be man's best friend also? Perhaps being a dog's best friend is a start in the right direction.

In man infantilism may also be related to the capacity for culture. There has certainly been a strong selection pressure in the human species favoring educability, or, in other words, the capacity to acquire information. The longer the period of infancy, the longer the time available for such learning. The humanistic psychologists Doctors Richard Alpert and Naomi Chenault go even further in considering personality development in relation to general systems theory, recommending an open system personality model. A closed personality system is regarded as one that is not mature, but, rather fixated at one development stage—and this is a rigid, inflexible type. The open personality system, providing flexibility and growth space, is a characteristic potential of man and it is related to his infantilism. In essence, man—the eternal child—never reaches maturity. It is his *culture* that makes him "mature" or level off and become stuck at one stage of development, and so freezes him into a closed system.

The whole concept of maturity, therefore, needs modifying. Consider the human brain: It is an incredibly flexible organ. Unlike the dog, man as a mature individual can learn an infinite variety of new tricks. Most animals, when they attain maturity, can learn only a few or, in a more scientific sense, they are less flexible. Their capacity to modify their behaviour or to elaborate new behaviour is very limited: Their personalities are in essence closed systems. Man's uniqueness and true potential lie in his neotenous brain—and in the openness of this system. A mature man perennially has the capacity to acquire new needs, goals, values, and to *unlearn* as well as to learn. Nonhuman animals operate more as a closed system with only a few basic needs and goals. They tend to come with strategies wired in a large array of instincts or blueprints, and their circuits are "hard-wired" as opposed to the more flexible "soft wiring" of the human brain. In man the period of plasticity, of flexibility, is not limited exclusively to infancy; we find a neurological infantilism still operating long after physical and sexual maturity have been reached. It provides a capacity for increasing knowledge, for acquisition of new ideas, and for expansion and rapid evolution of the culture within a single generation, or even less.

Infantilism in relation to an open neuropsychic apparatus in the adult may be related to creative genius, and we can identify at least two types. One is the dependent type who need society's external support and reward, and who is often subject to moods of depression, paranoia, and fear of rejection. Often such individuals have very indulgent parents. The other type is the self-reinforcing, self-actualizing paedomorph. He has his own internal support and reward mechanisms. He can operate, create, and continue to develop essentially independent of his culture. He does not rely on others for accolades. In fact, he is often *oblivious* to success. In his own lifetime he may be branded as a social deviant or as an eccentric outcast.

Neoteny, infantilism, or paedomorphosis has great significance in relation to man's development as a cultural being. It is clearly a double-edged sword—at once an attribute and a danger. And it may well be one of the prime routes of access to political manipulation and domination of the masses for controllers who reinforce dependency and insecurity.

But in relation to the human mind this capacity for unlimited growth and reorganization in the fully mature individual is man's key to the universe. Jesus Christ said that unless you become as a little child, you cannot enter the kingdom of heaven. Pathological regression to an infantile state is not what is being implied here, but rather a process of purification of mind and spirit, so that a person attains again the culturally unbiased clarity of an infant. This can be done by shucking off many acquired habits and the roles, rituals and façades man acquires from his society. Once he can free himself from culturally imposed limitations and repressions, he can perhaps regain the purity and innocence of a child. And when this is integrated with the knowledge acquired over a lifetime, he is a more complete or actualizing human being. In such a state he is in a far better condition to contribute significantly to the welfare of his own kind and to improve the culture in which he lives, as well as himself.

The child motif in mystical terms has been employed for centuries. It is an archetype—an image of purity and innocence uncontaminated by selfish, materialistic, and worldly interests. Reality is perceived with a clear, spontaneous, unbiased vision. In order to regain this vision a person has to unlearn much of what he has acquired, in the negative sense, from his culture. The essence of becoming "as a little child" again is regaining one's paedomorphic or neotenous potential for continued growth, continued integration, and greater awareness of one's purpose in life and life's meaning and fulfillment. Clare Owens, in an article in *Main Currents in Modern Thought,* regards the mystical state essentially as a regression to an earlier pre-infantile level of consciousness. This level is recognized as the Jungian collective unconscious, which she suggests is the core of one's sense of being. It is here that the seeds of creativity lie, as well as feelings of inner harmony, integrity, and unity with mankind. This state, quite different from the symbiotically unitive consciousness of the infant, suggests an integrative and universal quality of the mature human mind.

It must be added that part of the mystical experience may include the sense of being surrounded by an exploding, intense light, and of energy vibrating in one's body. Perhaps this recalls the moment of birth, but whatever its origins, it can be an intense and meaningful experience beyond words. Owens goes on to say we should encourage the integrative education of children to teach them they are part of the universal continuum that Einstein found to be a reality. This is a truth all mystics have known. The mystical state, whether spontaneous or induced through meditation or other practices, produces a release of energy from the unconscious that allows the actualization of man's highest potentialities. Therefore, Owens says, it seems proper that the mystic state should be studied by science without prejudice in an effort to discover whether it may indeed offer clues to the good life for the individual and for society. In the frame of our present discussion the mystic state* is regarded as a release of energies dammed up as a consequence of society's repressive influences that cause a fossilization of development or fixation at an immature stage—a stage the general populace may even regard as the ultimate level of maturity. In essence, it is a release from entropy, a freeing of one's growth potential. It is important for all of us to become aware of the imposed limitations in our lives and to find our own ways of liberation.

---

* Which is really not mystically unearthly and unreal, but simply a particular state of perfectly normal and healthy consciousness.

5

Animal and Human Displays:
Skin, Fur, and Clothes

That man wears clothes would seem to separate him from animals. On the contrary, clothes either exaggerate the animal within us or conceal it. Some of the similarities between human clothes and the furry or feathery display structures of animals can give us a clearer understanding of human nature and sometimes even a glimpse of the unconscious as well as conscious psyche of the wearer!

Primitive man, lacking an insulating layer of body fur, used the skins or furs of various animals as clothing and to build protective shelters. Later he developed skills of spinning and weaving, and used both plant and animal materials to make protective and insulating materials. Perhaps, early on, the ablest hunter girded himself with the finest skins of the animals that were hardest to kill. The notion of status revealed by what he wore emerged, and this was soon reinforced by additional adornments of animal, vegetable, or mineral origin. In many regions where the climate was mild, clothes were not necessary, but the body was still decorated with artifacts and covered uniformly with dust or ashes or painted or tattooed in various patterns. Artifacts most rare or dangerous to obtain endowed status on the wearer; painted or tattooed designs took on symbolic form, and together with particular adornments—feathered headgear, masks

Even though the superficial similarities between animal and man may be coincidental, man is still an animal within. He differs only in degree from others, whom he might see as inferior, and in the degree to which he can conceal his own faults and weaknesses.

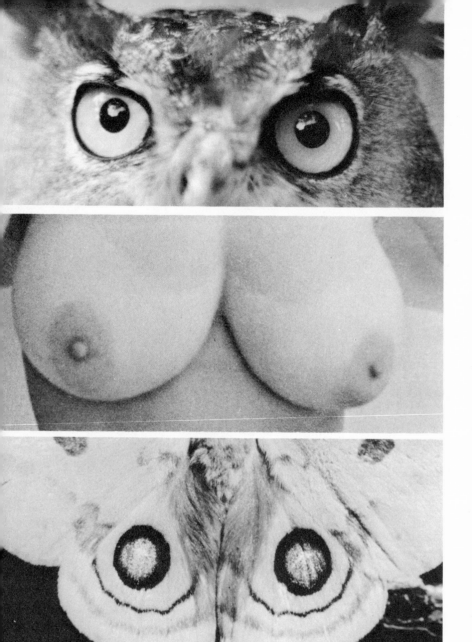

Analogous display structure. Eyes can threaten and mesmerize; "eye" spots on moth's wings are a warning to birds that it is poisonous; "eye" spots of areolae of the human breast give a potent visual-orienting signal.

resembling a special animal or unknown and feared (mythological) beasts, were incorporated into tribal ritual. In those associated with fertility rites, war ceremonies, and so on, body ornaments were employed as part of an increasingly symbolic and stereotyped tradition. These ceremonials were often accompanied by music, singing, and dancing, in which the sounds and movements mimicked human actions or those of animals that were especially revered, hunted, or feared.

Quite independent of the purely utilitarian value of clothing, it is clear that body adornment endowed the wearer with social identity or status, protection against evil, sickness, or other misfortune (talisman); or with certain characteristics of the totem animal (strength, speed, bravery). While, additionally, artifacts common to the tribe were associated with social cohesion or group identification and group ritual. Wearing an animal's fur (or feathers) also helped to conceal men while hunting, and possibly by wearing this camouflage and copying the animal's behaviour, the hunter could stalk close to his prey. Consequently he became at once actor and ethologist, learning how to "read" animals, how to hunt and capture them, and how to avoid being caught or injured in the process. Part of this knowledge of animal behaviour (e.g., courtship displays, prey stalking, or threat postures) and of animal plumage, was incorporated into tribal dances and rites. And the hunter might grossly exaggerate the plumage or behaviour pattern or refine and modify it as it was handed down from generation to generation.

Also imaginary animals conjured up by incomprehensible sounds and shadowy shapes in the dark jungle or in the sea or skies, came to life in ritual costumes and dances; a well-known example is the head mask of the dragon, its body an undulating sequence of dancers central to modern-day celebrations in the Orient.

Looking now at the adornments of Western man, we can easily identify certain "primitive" or ancestral patterns, namely ceremonial (wedding, funeral) and tribal-professional (city suit, "common identity," and uniform designs), which more subtly carry social status in the quality of material and the cut, "taste" being

A chimpanzee who hunted, killed, and ate a bush buck wears its skin all day in a "detached ecstatic" state.

a national phenomenon with few regional variations. The uniformity is in part determined by advertisements that suggest to the consumer there is status in adopting the latest fashions and hairstyles, no matter how bizarre. Add to this the individual's innate fear of not being acceptable to the group majority, the fear of being nonconformist, and we see the campus students and young people, who react against society by being nonconformist, adopting a group conformist costume and behaviour.*

Western man has also developed specific uniforms associated with professional roles—the whites and greens of nurses and doctors (the latter with the intern's badge, the perennial stethoscope); the utilitarian pale or dark blue, or khaki worker's clothes; and the specific colors of the various military forces, to which are added various insignia demoting regiment, rank, past valor, length of career, and campaign service.

Military uniforms are clearly "living fossils" of earlier tribal adornments; even the regimental badge (and the actual mascot used on parade) may be an eagle or a panther that protects or endows its wearer with its strength. The power of such a symbolic insignia or talisman is not lost when the symbol is not an animal; crossed swords or a mailed fist are symbols of group identity and may still have considerable value in psychologically "protecting" their wearer. An insignia such as the swastika may instill fear in the enemy or in the persecuted, while the cross or the Star of David may inspire hope in the persecuted or mark them for destruction. It is in the ethological sense an acquired releaser of feelings, such as militant enthusiasm, patriotism, or allegiance to the company. A number of uniforms have also been evolved for particular regiments, all carrying the same basic insignia. But uniforms for combat have less revealing badges of valor, rank, or regiment, and may be more cryptically coloured to enhance camouflage than the elaborate full dress used for ceremonial occasions. In fact, the mottled "disruptive" gray-green patterns used to camouflage battle dress closely resemble those seen in cryptically coloured animals. Colour and pattern make

---

* But they may well be aware of the difference between the uniformity of conformity and the uniformity of a deeper unity.

the body "blend" with the background, as the actual body contours are subtly eliminated. Similarly, in sports, various teams have basic practical uniforms for competition and often a separate one or a blazer for display of the club's emblem: Again, an animal symbol or totem may be used, either to imply certain qualities of speed and strength—the "Bears," the "Tigers"—or to denote a regional characteristic—a cardinal or a long-horned steer. Few symbolic adornments are used by nonmilitary and nonsporting Western man; engagement and wedding rings, "going steady" teenage eternity rings, and fraternity pins adorning sorority girls are the most common. Others include discreet military or club insignia, personal insignia like initialed tie tacks, and personal-sentimental, beautifying or status-signifying jewelry.

Additional adornments include hand (nails), eye, and mouth makeup in the female, powders and creams to lend youthful bloom to the skin, nylon stockings to smooth and shape the legs, and girdles and bras to accentuate breasts, waist, and hips. Primitive tribes employ splints and coils to set off earlobes, nostrils, neck, or lips, and may additionally decorate the body with patterned incisions that are treated to prolong healing and enhance the growth of keloid scar tissue.

Western women also use surgery to improve their looks—cosmetic surgery to bob the nose or perk the breasts, tattoolike procedures to remove superfluous hair, chemical (silicone) or hormonal injections to enlarge the breasts or buttocks and plastic surgery to pare them down. Tight skirts render the stride short and daintily feminine, while the high-heeled shoe makes the foot appear smaller (not a bound foot, praise be!) and the leg more elegant. The tight skirt is reminiscent of one tribal custom of "hobbling" the female like a horse so she cannot, symbolically, run away.

All these, coupled with alluring or revealing clothes, give an additional dimension to body adornment—not for sexual identification by the natural insignia afforded by bare breasts and buttocks, but for the attraction or seduction of the opposite sex. Such pains, such extremes, and yet it is taboo to touch or to look at another male's mate. Is her display now so ritualized and far removed from its original motivation of sexual attraction that it is merely a status symbol of his virility for her mate, or is it pure narcissism? The female certainly dresses to compete with other females. Perhaps every woman would like to strip and tease. Perhaps not. It is more probable that if she does not expose the precise expanse of chest and thigh that fashion dictates, she feels alienated from the group; so, to avoid this, she conforms. Are modest virgins blackmailed, or are they more likely to lure a future mate by exposing their wares? Some may wear certain "fetish" materials—black underwear, leather or rubber, or tight, leopard-spotted clothes. These are also the delights of the transvestite and the display structures of the homosexuals who assume feminine roles and who can so often superbly mimic female behaviour patterns. What observant, if rather specialized, ethologists they are!

Both male and female increase their social acceptability in some cultures by removing or masking natural body odours with mouthwash and deodorant.* Natural body odour may be an important sexual stimulus and its reduction may increase social distance. Is it a necessary adaptive device under crowded work conditions? Strong body odour of one male may intimidate another (or nauseate a plastic, denaturalized, vaginally deodorized female). The sheer intensity of the synthetic perfume trail the female leaves as she passes can be a potent stimulus to the male to follow her with his eyes. But he might sneeze or gag instead, and such physiological reactions can enable him to distinguish a "cheap" female from a more sophisticated one, even in total darkness, on the basis of the quality of her perfume. Eastern perfumes, heavy with musk, may mimic if not exaggerate the female odour, and prove highly arousing.† Such "hypertrophy" of olfactory signals compensates for a reduction of visual signals if the female's body is draped in shapeless clothing and her face veiled.

---

* Removal of hair from the legs, armpits, and upper lip in Western females is common practice and may be intended to make the body seem more youthful or infantile. In other cultures such practices are not followed because hair is associated with maturity, fertility, and sexuality in the female.

† Dr. Richard Michael has recently isolated a pheromone (copulin) from the vaginas of female monkeys which causes immediate sexual arousal in males.

With only half the body covered (and artfully supported) many females are more attractive or alluring than they would be in the nude. Perhaps this is why man associates night and darkness with lovemaking, when he need only touch his spouse and imagine, rather than confront cold reality. The shock of seeing a bride removing prosthetic breasts and other alluring deceits must be traumatic. Premarital sex clearly has its place; truth will out.

But the male is not beyond reproach either. He now bleaches and waves his hair, may sport a toupee, struts in elevated shoes and swings padded shoulders accentuated by a tapered waist and tightly clad legs. Modern "tasteful" tailoring once de-emphasized what some now emphasize in tight slacks. The padded jockstrap that is nowadays associated with the male-exaggerating homosexual was once the Brueghelian codpiece of the virile male. The cockscomb and the fop added further padding* to less vital areas like thighs, calves, shoulders, and arms, and accentuated gestures with frills and the flourishing of kerchiefs and monocles; the sword, once a weapon, dwindled to a mere shadow symbol of masculinity, the elegant walking stick.

Removal of the beard is more enigmatic. In the adolescent it is a sign of virility, while its removal in the adult may help in preserving a youthful appearance, creating the illusion of youthful virility. Or is the removal of the beard (a sexual characteristic), together with careful tailoring at the crotch and application of deodorants yet another example of the reduction of male sex signals in Western man's attempt to adapt to crowded conditions by de-emphasizing sexual (and competitive-aggressive) stimuli.

In nature, we see comparable examples in social animals. The male plumage acts first as a territorial or individual sex-identity flag against rival males and, second, attracts females. Do we have a reversal of this phenomenon in the two sexes of the human species? As a general rule the male is usually a "super-male" in terms of size and display adornments in polygamous species like

---

* Comparable padding is seen in many animals to give an illusion of size, such as the mane of the lion and bison and the deep chest (dewlap) of a goat or bull.

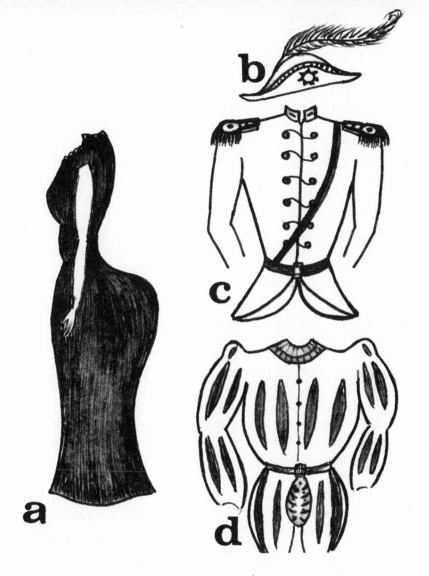

As in the evolution of display structures in animals to enhance status, sexuality, and communication, so the evolution of human costumes follows analogous patterns. (a) Although the covered body reveals no flesh, exaggerated padding and corseting compensate to create a supra-feminine profile. (c) Military tunic, with epaulettes, cut-in waist, and front buttons, gives an impressive frontal (threat) display and illusion of broad powerful shoulders. (b) The plumed hat denotes status and enhances stature. (d) Pleated and puffed vest and pants exaggerate flamboyant movements, and the padded and embroidered codpiece advertises potency to all.

the moose and elephant seal, while in monogamous species like the coyote and wolf, males more closely resemble females.

Such a paradox: Sexual sign stimuli are either emphasized or de-emphasized. Liberal emphasis of sexuality often contradicts social taboos or inhibitions. A subtle process may be operating in which exaggeration of certain sexual sign stimuli has a positive effect on social organization and integration. A simple example: A shapely female will more surely draw a male audience into conversation than a female who looks or behaves asexually. A male is more polite, more attentive, and her "feminine" solicitous behaviour charms him and supports his masculine ego, so he carries her suitcase (may chivalry never die—only chauvinism!).

In some species the male mimics the female genitalia, or vice versa. The enlarged and reddened posterior of the female hamadryas baboon is mimicked by the male. In the spotted hyena the female mimics the male in that she has a pseudopenis. Oddities? Obscure examples? Certainly, but they illustrate the point that such sign stimuli can play a major role in social behaviour, as communication signals that may facilitate the maintenance of sexual identity and group cohesion. Apropos of the codpiece alluded to earlier, some primitive tribesmen wear a long gourd tied in an erect position over the penis, which may be a sexual and status display comparable to an analogous phenomenon in some monkey species, notably the squirrel monkey. The dominant male performs a social display, employing a specific body posture to enhance a sustained penile erection. Other primates have evolved bright colours to emphasize the genitalia; the scrotum (and often the buttocks) is blue and the penis red, and it is perhaps no coincidence that the face of the male mandrill is also coloured blue and red. The evolution of this penis-face phenomenon is intriguing; colours become more intense as the male matures. Some ethologists have compared it to the practice of making up the face with various pigments in the human female. Both the pigtailed capuchin and the Western woman share blue eyelids. The red lips of the human female may mimic the vulva, and the rouged cheeks may mimic the breasts. The buttocks in turn may mimic the breasts, and the breasts are accentuated by

Sexual display as a sign of status in male mandrill and a Masai warrior who places a swagger stick between his legs. Tribesmen of New Guinea highlands place long gourds over their genitals for the same purpose.

the eyespotlike areolae, which clearly catch the eye. Such analogies are based on flimsy evidence and other arguments are more convincing. The buttocks may mimic the breasts, but only in their youthful firmness and line. In some native tribes the female buttocks are especially attractive to the male, and they may be hypertrophied with fat deposits—a "stored" supply of food in adaptation to an ecology where food is seasonally scarce—at a time when children have to be nurtured. Similarly, the breast adds to its primary purpose—providing milk—a secondary function as a sex signal, and indeed the most sexually attractive breasts are not necessarily the best suited to nursing, because the infant may have great difficulty in seizing the teat and in breathing while sucking.

Makeup of the eyes and mouth may act merely to accentuate those facial structures that are of direct communication value in expressing a woman's emotions or feelings. A beauty spot or applied mole serves merely to orient, to catch the eye, and is comparable to the breast areolae (and possibly the navel or umbilicus, where a jewel might be placed). Similar effects are produced by inserting a jewel in the nostril or a mark on the forehead. Rouge on the cheeks obviously implies a healthy and youthful complexion, more so than it mimics the breasts.

Perfume applied to the erotogenic areas, earrings and the earlobes themselves, lipstick and the lips themselves, the areolae, and the axillary and pubic hair all act as stimuli to highlight the erotogenic zones and to orient and direct the mate's behaviour. Body odours (pheromones) from the axillary and genital regions may also arouse and orient behaviour. (The facial beard of the male may in sexual play provide added stimulation to these erotogenic regions.)

And now we turn to human nakedness and the "shame" or embarrassment of being seen naked. The church was quick to exploit the human fear of being naked—fear triggered by the complete loss of all the socially ingrained attitudes discussed earlier. This natural social fear was translated into shame, so that greater control over sexual and social behaviour might be achieved. It became sinful for woman to display herself in public, and long dresses covered all, while the male replaced such symbols of masculinity as his sword and codpiece with a walking stick or cross. So it was with the Puritans.

To compensate for this prohibition against nakedness the bustle and exaggerated corsetry emerged to emphasize the buttocks, waist, and hips: Breasts were later elevated on platforms almost at chin height. Elaborate wigs, facial makeup and emotive, coquettish fans also appeared. Later the "stovepipe" style came in—dresses were sheer and shapeless, and breasts were flattened. Soon the unaccentuated body was again accentuated by "plunging" necks and backs, see-through blouses where unsupported breasts and unaccentuated waist and loins revealed themselves as the body moved against a clinging veil, each vital area visible beneath shimmering sequins. So it was in the roaring twenties. Comparing the various costumes throughout the ages,* we see a general rule emerging, especially in the female. The more completely the body is covered, the more hidden parts are exaggerated by padding, corseting, or intimacy of cloth with skin. Also, parts left exposed, such as the head, face, arms, and legs are more lavishly decorated with jewels, cosmetics, and hosiery.

Artful, semirevealing adornment can clearly be more arousing than the actual flaccid body beneath in all its nakedness. Many religious sects, like the Puritans, have recognized this and enforced the wearing of the least arousing or revealing clothes possible. Clothes were sexually monomorphic, or identical, in terms of color: Sexual dimorphism, or distinctive differences, were reduced, no facial makeup was used, and the hair was plastered in a severe bun or hidden beneath a cap. Their prohibitions were directed at the sinful bacchanalian revelries of the time. Desires of the flesh were buried beneath clothes and behind demurely downcast eyes, subdued by earnest prayer.

It has been suggested that the padded shoulders of the female during World War II developed to suggest greater strength (and equality) on the part of the female in a time of national crisis.

---

* Several authors have commented that the style of costume at a given time in history often closely matches the styles of architecture and interior decoration.

Civilian clothes assumed certain military lines (Eisenhower jackets, trench coats, and leather boots became high couture).

National and international affairs obviously have a profound effect on both social behaviour and the adornment patterns of the female and, perhaps to a lesser extent, the male. The changes tend to be cyclic, with variations or epicycles attributable to economic, moral-religious, and other social influences. More recently the influence of advertising in promoting annual changes in style has created a lucrative, if ridiculously superfluous industry. Merchandising techniques can be so effective that society may accept a new product or style that in no way reflects its needs or tastes. This accounts for the acceptance of very unfeminine (or unappealing to the male) clothes by females exposed to modern advertising propaganda: They don't really want it, but it's "the latest thing" and they conform. On the other hand, market or consumer research can probe deeply into human psychology, and when suitably promoted, the products of such research responding to deep-seated desires are an instant success (unless, of course, public taste changes overnight, as it so often does). A style like the miniskirt may need only a little advertising before it sweeps the country, for both display-determined females and target males are gratified. The product is psychologically acceptable and has been presented at a socioeconomically appropriate time. Curiously though, the "hot pants" craze only had a half-life of some three months.

Possibly the appearance of asexual fashions for the female that border on masculine or "little choirboy" styles—jackets, pants, shirts, ties, cropped hair, small breasts, and little or no makeup—do reveal a conspiracy on the part of homosexual dress designers. Do they seek gratification or find pleasure in defeminizing their customers? Such fashions ordinarily do not endure because the male population rejects them, but at times they can be promoted when advertising hits the younger set at the right moment. Promotion of a superstar like the rag trade's "Twiggy" (really a boyish Oliver Twist) set such a revolution in motion. But the effect was transitory for adults are sexually dimorphic and normally, therefore, prefer to be clearly distinguishable.

Is it mere speculation to suppose that as society evolves, stratifies, and fragments into ever-increasing complexity, individualized styles associated with age, sex, status, and role will give way to more uniform dress within subgroups or "castes"? At the time of writing, social complexity seems to have reached an unprecedented peak and is reflected in the rich variety of styles that are now socially acceptable, styles ranging from careful corporate conservatism to the flamboyant gear of liberated homosexuals. Such minority group uniformity could have the effect of diminishing social distance. It is exemplified today in the patched, blue jean "unisex" gear of male and female students and in the ageless and sexless uniforms of the People's Republic of China. Similarly, the monk's habit, for example, is less a uniform or badge (except to people outside the order) than a unifying style designed to exert a positive social influence on the brethren: Age, role, and status are eliminated, and external displays that might lead to status conflict and hierarchical rivalry are removed.

James Laver, in a Zoological Society of London symposium on the natural history of aggression, has discussed some intriguing aspects of the influence of costume on human behaviour (and vice versa). He stresses first that class distinctions are made with stratification of culture into "castes" or classes and clothes displaying one's status and success: then there is further distinction between utilitarian and ornamental clothes, work clothes, and fine clothes. Laver refers to this as the hierarchical principle. The female might be adorned by her mate to display his success, but she also dresses to attract, something Laver labels the seduction principle. The utility principle, Laver further suggests, tends to counterbalance the other two. It should be emphasized that at any given period in the history of the evolution of costumes, all three principles may be identified, but one is particularly exaggerated by the transient dictates of fashion.

Laver equates the wearing of status clothes with an assertion of status, and therefore sees it as a means of social aggresion. At one time people were not allowed to wear clothes that were above their social status. Aristocratic clothes eloquently proclaimed that their wearer did not *need* to work. The white-cuff, white-collar executive of today, whose status is above the blue-collar worker, is a living remnant of the aristocrat sporting enormous lace ruffs round neck and wrists (Laver's antiutility principle). No one could possibly work in such restricting finery!

It seems that as styles evolve, they reach a point of extreme exaggeration, and like their counterparts in animals, they eventually become extinct or, more usually, persist as token remnants, rather like the "just right amount of white cuff" today's executive displays. After the French Revolution aristocratic costumes (the elaborate eighteenth-century courtier's paraphernalia) gave way to the more democratic dress of the gentleman, dress that nevertheless still maintained the hierarchical principle. The gentlefolk, in contrast to the working classes, wore stylized clothes that, as Laver lucidly observes, declared that their wearer was an English country gentleman who rode horses. The distinctive features of cut and cloth served to maintain the hierarchical principle when the lower classes mimicked these styles.

This era then gave way to the "sporting" period, when country clothes—easy and comfortable—emerged. These combined the utilitarian with the hierarchical principle to display that the wearer did not have to work, although he *was* an active person. Laver points out that the lower classes often took on the styles the upper classes discarded; thus the footman wore the costume of the courtier, and later, the waiter wore that of the frock-coated gentleman. Modern "sports clothes" mimic skiing, mountaineering, and golfing costumes (zipper jackets, windbreakers, and tight slacks); fishing clothes (polo or turtleneck sweaters); riding and hunting clothes (hacking and safari-style jackets). These are often combined with military or working styles, as exemplified by the present trend of young people to wear battle-dress blouses and fatigues, or cowboy jackets and jeans. These comfortable clothes display that their wearer is active, sporty, and perhaps *ready* to work, though he or she might in fact be a lazy layabout. The costume of the communist Chinese—working clothes and cloth cap—clearly conforms to Laver's classifications; they are uniform, utilitarian, antihierarchical, and clearly non-

Makeup. . .

and costume for display!
Photos: Herb Whitman

seductive. But some status is still maintained by the leaders who adorn them with tiny tin stars.

It is interesting that Dr. James Laver of the Victoria and Albert Museum in London* finds it easier to make social distinctions between European males than females on the basis of their dress. The former is not so true in America, where males of all classes tend to wear comfortable, sporty working-type clothes. The wealthy man (who might instead decorate his wife) often wears strikingly out-of-place casual clothes; this is an antihierarchical principle, that might be an inverted way of demonstrating status. The lower-class American male tends to overdress, in ironic contrast to the calculated casualness of the wealthy. In between this is the Ivy League college look, in which both male and female mimic the sporty country-tweed look of the British.

Laver concludes that with mass production of clothes, greatly reducing their cost, the hierarchical principle is breaking down. Class distinctions are disappearing and marriage across class lines may then be promoted. He believes that women's clothes of today have abandoned the hierarchical principle (although this might not be true *within* the sex, for female will compete with female) and that they represent a fairly stable balance between the seduction and utility principles. He maintains that men have not recovered much of the seduction principle in their dress, which represents the rearguard action of the hierarchical principle against the growing advance of the utility principle.

A few ethologists like Paul Leyhausen and Otto Koenig have studied some aspects of dress in terms of the "releasing value" of certain costume's component parts. For example, there is a close correlation between some aspects of military uniforms and attitudes of threat. Epaulets and elbow pads emphasize the hunched shoulder, elbows-out threat posture, enhanced by clenched, gloved fists. A hat may emphasize stature, epaulets and the cut of the tunic and braid on the chest may suggest intimidating shoulder width. A black hat is apparently more menacing than a white one.

---

* Also see J. Laver, "Costume as a Means of Social Aggression" in J. D. Carthy and F. J. Ebling (eds.), *The Natural History of Aggression,* Academic Press, 1964.

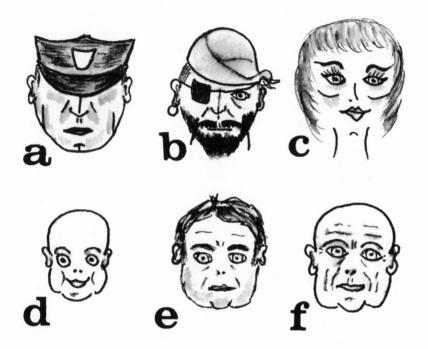

Sunglasses, a low, shining visor or cap front (a) serve to conceal and therefore increase control and threat by increasing social distance. (b) An eye patch and moustache similarly increase distance and control by concealment, and the single eye has an intimidating assymetry. (c) Makeup exaggerates eye size and softens the skin, both infantile nonaggressive signals, now incorporated into the smooth "paedomorphic" sexuality of the human female. (d-f) The loss of hair and other 'helpless' attitudes that accompany aging may mimic the nonthreatening, care-evoking qualities of infancy.

Soldiers are trained to tuck their chins in, a basic threat position commonly seen in animals in aggressive encounters. This military display may be enhanced by a chin strap and a small peak on the hat that sticks out horizontally just above the eyes like a great, frowning eyebrow. This is supported by Leyhausen's findings that on the medieval soldier model he used in his studies, thick eyebrows were definitely intimidating.

The costumes of today's youth provide a rich source of speculation. The "unisex" look; the Eastern mystic (caftans), the American Indian (ponchos), and Jewish kibbutz (coveralls) look; the worn, patched (often ex-military) secondhand "recycled" ecological look*—through these styles individuals identify with the youth movement, with the youth international. Clothing again becomes an eloquent expression, be it political, social, or both.

Modern male clothing is more flamboyant, and perhaps we are at last seeing a return of the seduction principle. This "flowery gear" may also be a reaction against utilitarian-military styles. Perhaps a man feels less pressure to display his status and masculinity now that the male ego can accept on equal terms the emancipated, creative female. "Unisex" may be a subtle indication that "male," "female," "husband," "wife," "mother," and "father" roles are no longer so clearly definable. The father is no longer ridiculed if he carries, cuddles, and feeds his baby in public. Nor is the mother criticized if she leaves her child with her husband or at a daycare center in order to engage in some creative activity outside the home. Only a few years ago such a professional woman would de-emphasize her seductive feminine displays and wear essentially utilitarian clothes. But she is now freer to wear and do what she likes. Both sexes are also having more fun with their bright, cheaply made clothes that last only for a single washing, if that. We may be moving into the anticipated era of disposable paper-synthetic clothes. Little of the hierarchical principle is visible in young people's clothing, with the exception

---

* And high couture doesn't miss out on this market. Embroidered and studded blue jean pants and jackets made of blue denim patches sell for hundreds of dollars in the late nineteen seventies: The hierarchial principle becomes superimposed on the utility principle!

of the occasional pair of fine cowhide pants and suede jacket that should now be much cheaper as demand escalates production. Some of their costumes give the false impression of the utilitarian principle; some wear work clothes of the lower classes and especially of peasants (Mexican style is extremely popular), many of these styles being the legacy of Peace Corps and kibbutz volunteers who've brought back from foreign countries something tangible and expressive often of newly acquired values as well.

A final poignant and amusing note concerns the current style of America's lower and middle middle-class women. They spend many hours having their hair teased and tortured into an enormous, stiff, bouffant confection (often tinted in various colours) reminiscent of the aristocratic wigs of eighteenth-century courtiers. And with this they wear a comfortable, utilitarian sports outfit (bowling alley chic) of sweater (pink) slacks (turquoise), ankle socks (white), and sneakers or low-heeled shoes. Over *this* they zipper a nylon "ski-golf" jacket. Above the neck they are ready for the ballroom (or is this simply status display?), while below it they purport to be ready for indoor suburban sports.

It will be interesting to follow the development of styles over the next few years in our youth-dominated Western culture. The world is shrinking; more young people travel to foreign countries today and enjoy sharing and wearing national costumes, while blue jeans have become a multinational, unifying symbol. Perhaps the age of nationalism is breaking down as a sense of worldly brotherhood takes root in our minds and is expressed overtly in values and dress alike.

6

The Skin Trade:
Wild Furs and Murder

Thumbing idly through *Vogue* and the *New Yorker* en route to the West Coast on a jumbo jet, I am between lectures—a morning one in Chicago to the Humane Society of the United States and a three-hour stint on an extension program at UCLA for people interested in animal behaviour. I feel tired but believe that what I am doing will help draw people closer to kinship with all life and, from this sense of the earth, make them more responsible stewards of this small spaceship.

Coats and trims of Russian marmot, fisher, Norwegian fox, American lynx, raccoon, opossum, squirrel (not to mention snakeskin belts and purses and wild-boar-hide shoes) adorn models in vacant, studied poses on glossy pages. These items are made from the furs and skins of wild-caught animals, as distinct from ranch-raised mink and fox: They are called "natural," meaning taken from the wild. Not taken like wild berries, but *poisoned, shot,* and *trapped.* Where are those real people who wear fake furs? We forget too easily and too soon. Every woman deserves perfection at least once on this earth, says the typical ad: But in wearing the perfect pelt, she unwittingly reveals man's major imperfection—inhumanity.

If the vibrations, the emotions of a trapped wild animal, were to remain in these furs, no human being could *ever* wear them. Use your imagination to project into these furs the truth—the criminal reality—of this unnecessary slaughter of wild animals to satisfy human vanity. They are contaminated, unclean, and unworthy adornments for our sisters of the earth. They are for the dead in mind and spirit, who display their ignorance adorned in the vain luxury of wild fur—wild fur which, in its richness and softness, stifles the scream of man's inhumanity to his fellow creatures. Wild animals have no rights, but the trappers claim *their* right to kill them, which they would never do if everyone simply refused to buy what the trappers rip off from nature, from small bodies still warm and sometimes even still *alive*.

Perhaps this says something of human values—that what you do and how you appear are more important than what you are or how you feel *inside*. Hollow, empty people wearing masks and playing games with no center of self appropriately wear hollow, emptied animals—their skins and pelts. (Perhaps if we ate their insides it would be better, but we are not that hungry yet.)

Trappers claim they are only taking the "surplus," and that by keeping the numbers down they prevent overpopulation and possible starvation and large-scale declines in wild animal populations. States and federal wildlife managers, who sometimes keep careful records, will set quotas to prevent overkill, and they agree that it is ecologically safe, perhaps even sound practice, to remove this "surplus." No trapper or bounty hunter would overkill anyway, they maintain, since he would be putting himself out of business.

What the trappers say, however, is nonsense. In areas where intensive hunting, trapping, and poisoning are done the target animals produce *more* offspring. They adapt to human predation; and the trappers are not doing the animals a service by removing the so-called natural surplus: They are, in fact, creating the surplus. If not "harvested" in this way but left alone, their population would soon naturally readjust.

Most of these furbearing animals are not shot because, unless

Choral singing in the wolf is a social ritual which differs little from the same social phenomenon in man, who would kill the wolf for sport and his own kind, as well without reason.
Photo: Herb Whitman

the hunter is an expert marksman, a shot would damage the pelt. Instead, they are poisoned with excruciatingly painful agents like strychnine or, more likely they are caught in a trap. A trap doesn't injure the pelt, since one or two feet are caught in the steel jaws— jaws that cut into bone and hold the animal in continued agony until it is shot through the head or clubbed to death (clubbing doesn't injure the pelt). Sometimes the terrified animal will struggle and literally tear itself apart trying to get free, ripping and biting its trapped foot. If it does escape, it may survive, but if in a state of shock, severely crippled and unable to get food or to fend for itself, it goes into hiding and dies.

Other times a larger animal—a dog, coyote, or wolf—will come and kill and eat the trapped animal. A merciful end, but a source of frustration to the trapper. Some are only weekend opportunists attending their traplines every six or seven days. Imagine how long some animals wait in the trap—perhaps two or three weeks if bad weather prevents the man from going out —before they are killed, or die of exposure. And an animal with a poor-quality pelt isn't skinned—just thrown away, destroyed for no purpose.

All this suffering for one end, one purposeless purpose: that people might wear wild furs.

Do you know that some states have bounties on bobcats, lynx, fox, coyote, and other animals and pay people to kill them? It is inconceivable to me that in this day and age any wild animal can be made into an outlaw and indiscriminately persecuted with a bounty on its head. It is like Hitler purging the Jews from his kingdom. A bounty is given to any species that takes farm live-stock, but much trapping and hunting occurs where there is no livestock, and the animals killed are innocent. Near farmlands some of their kind may kill an occasional lamb or chicken, but because of them the entire species is persecuted. Even if there *were* no bounties, though, wild animals will still be killed so long as there is a market for their fur and so long as sheep ranchers want a one hundred percent profit and regard all eagles and coyotes as enemies. (These animals probably save them millions

Wild North American lynx jacket and ranch fox coats attract buyers who ignorantly indulge themselves.

of dollars annually by controlling rabbits and small rodents that would otherwise eat the grass intended for their sheep.)

Men and women seeking liberation from their own societal roles may well identify with being used and not taken for what they are when they see that man "uses" not just people, but fur-bearing animals—in fact the whole of nature for his own ends. The world and your life, too, will be different when we begin to see each other for what we are, rather than in terms of how we might use or otherwise exploit each other and the world around us.

Next time you see an ad in a magazine or the furs of wild animals for sale in a local store, complain. Let the immorality be known. Many store managers are innocent, as are most of those who wear such furs or who would contemplate purchase. Tell them the truth, dispel their ignorance, and replace their dangerous innocence with awareness.

Finally, a distinction between ranch-raised and wild-caught natural furs. Raccoon, ocelot, margay, opossum, beaver, deer, lynx, marmot, fisher, seal, and squirrel are taken from the wild. Others, notably mink, chinchilla, and sometimes foxes, are raised on ranches. Mink and chinchilla adapt well and are akin to "farmed" animals such as sheep, pig, calf, and cow, which we eat and wear. But keeping relatively wild animals like foxes in captivity just for their fur is inhumane—think twice before buying ranch fox. If you wear mink or chinchilla, you might perhaps come into my home. But don't even think twice about buying a natural, wild animal fur or skin. If you do, you are condoning murder and supporting an industry that on moral, ecological, and humane grounds has no right to exist. We need food, not furs. Let the trappers raise chickens or corn or find some alternative source of income. Wild furs are a luxury, and such self-indulgence only serves to perpetuate that side of our nature which is inhuman and which could ultimately destroy us all. We must all begin to live together with each other and with nature and put an end to this ceaseless and needless exploitation and destruction.

7

Hunters and Humane Values

I know the satisfaction of tracking and shooting deer or wolves, and I have been with the hunters of whales and tigers. If I can, I shoot my animals not once but many times—I use a camera and my expertise is in animal behaviour and ecology.

People have been around for a long time. For the past ten thousand years they have been domesticating animals and plants, but for a hundred thousand years before that they were hunters. Today hunting societies are rare and, as with mastodons and sabre-toothed tigers, are on the way out. But because in our ancestry we spent so many generations as hunters, many of us today still feel the need to go out into the wild to satisfy this ancient drive. It takes skill and courage to track and kill big game, and stealth and experience to hunt wary, elusive animals like wolves and deer. The spirit of the hunter rises to meet such challenges, and success is one of the most gratifying experiences a man can hope for. To get a trophy specimen, or to bring good venison home for the family, is to relive the ancient rituals and experience again the pride and esteem our hunting ancestors once felt.

The psychology or mental apparatus of deer and wolf is quite different, and this is because each is adapted to a particular life-style. Similarly, in the early evolution of man, there was a divi-

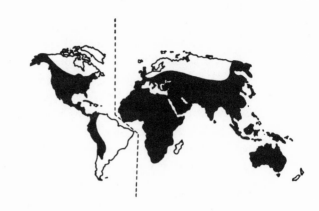

10,000 B.C.

World Population: 10 million
Per Cent Hunters: 100

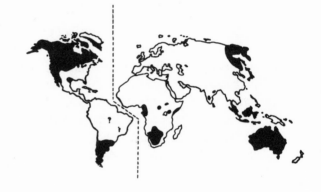

1500 A.D.

World Population: 350 million
Per Cent Hunters: 1.0

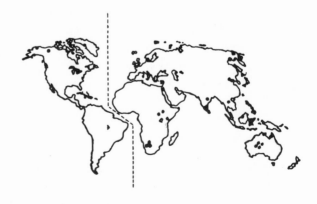

1900 A.D.

World Population 3 billion
Per Cent Hunters: 0.001

From Lee & DeVore, *Man the Hunter*.

sion of labor between the sexes. Man normally did the hunting
while women (and children) gathered plant foods—seeds, roots,
fruit, and so on, tended the camp, and prepared the meals. With
different roles the psychological makeup of the male began to
evolve differently from the female, and physical differences were
also evident, males being more muscular and fleet-of-foot than
females. Perhaps this is why today hunting is still basically a
male pastime. Although women's lib has helped break down the
ancient taboos of female exclusion from male hunting groups (as
in contemporary big game hunting associations), it may or may
not change a hundred thousand years or more of evolution. Natural and social selection made the egos of male and female different, each superbly adapted to a particular role—certainly a
highly efficient evolutionary solution to the problems of survival
of primitive man, who lacked both agriculture and technology.

Now we have both—so what of the human psyche today? Is
the male ego still allied to hunting and the female disposed to
gathering and preparing food? Anthropological studies of our
living ancestors, the "Stone Age" Australian aborigines and the
! Kung bushmen of the Kalahari desert in Africa, confirm that our
ancestors divided labor between the sexes and that it was the
male who hunted. Similarly, it is the man of modern society
rather than the woman who enjoys hunting; until recently, in
fact, it was almost considered deviant or pathological for a woman
to do so. A man's pleasure in leaving the city or suburban world
of conformity and uniformity to go into the country to hunt is
not just a good therapeutic break from everyday. It also gratifies
the male ego. Some psychoanalysts interpret this gratification as
sexual, seeing the gun as a phallus, while others read it as an
outlet for frustration and aggression.

It is unfortunate that such spokesmen know so little of human
anthropology. The gratification is clearly in hunting per se. A
few may find sexual gratification, but for most, surely, hunting
must be as sexually fulfilling as doing the laundry or waxing
the car. It is also unlikely that hunting is an outlet for aggresssion.
Some anti-hunters say, "Better let them shoot animals than shoot
us, which they would if there were no animals for them to shoot."

Even my colleagues, ethologists who study animal and human behaviour, tend to confuse aggressive and hunting behaviour. Watch any wolf or lion hunting and making a kill. No aggressive signals are given: It's simply hard, often dangerous work. The confusion comes because the animals and men use the same weapons and similar actions as they do in actual fighting. An animal or human when hunting, therefore, is turned on neither sexually nor aggressively—the motivation is to hunt and kill, not to breed or to fight, even though some of the actions may be allied and the brain centres involved intimately related. But now a few more words about aggression:

One of the world's most distinguished professors of animal behaviour, Nobel laureate and friend, Konrad Lorenz, has widely publicized his views that man is innately aggressive. Since aggression in animals may be vital to survival of the "fittest," aggression in man also has a survival function. The ability to respond aggressively (when territory or family are threatened) is thought to be innate or inborn. This is indeed true; there are brain centres that organize specific aggressive responses to certain incoming stimuli (which may be reflexlike releasers in less complex animals or learned in man). Lorenz's thesis breaks down, however, when he claims the existence of an inborn drive to aggress, comparable to the drive for food, for sex, or for care of young. An animal or person deprived of food or sex, or separated from loved ones will seek some solution to remedy the deprivation. But no normal animal or person will actively seek out a context in which to fight—there is no buildup in the face of fight deprivation, of a drive to aggress, as there is with the drive for food, sex, or social affiliation.

The pessimistic conclusion from his treatise on aggression in man is that it is innate, and therefore little can be done about it except through external conditioning or manipulation. What is wrong with humanity is not the basic nature of man but his nurture. Because of his enculturated bias, Lorenz falls perhaps naturally into the "nature" side of the nature versus nurture controversy, favoring the role of genes and instincts over experience in determining behaviour. He is surely too much a humanist and

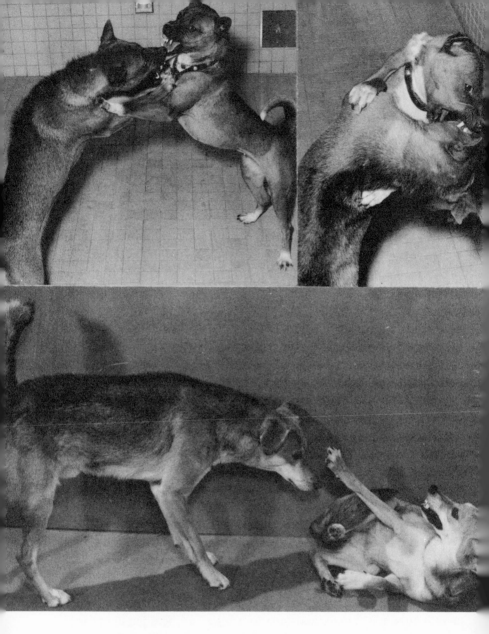

Ritualized fighting in dogs includes sparring, biting at a "safe" region (the check), and inhibiting an attack by assuming a submissive attitude of surrender. As in man, ritual control may break down and severe injuries may be inflicted.

Ritualized aggression in man, seen in ancient times in duelling and jousting, and in contemporary sports, too, which today may be one "safe" or acceptable outlet for aggression.

man of knowledge to hold such exclusive views, but he is naive enough through his own dogmatic thinking to fall into the "nature" side of the nature/nurture debate.

How an animal fights is basically determined through heredity; who it fights and when is determined more by hormones and experience (learning). The American psychobiologist John Paul Scott clearly states the holistic casual sequence: Genes plus training produce aggressivity; aggressivity plus stimulation produce aggression.

We know that some genetic strains of mice can be trained or stimulated to fight more easily than others. They seem to have a lower threshold than others—a shorter fuse—before they fight. The same is true of various breeds of dog, some, like bull terriers, having been selectively bred for fighting.

Training and stimulation (provocation) are also important, and such environmental influences (nurture) are no less significant than the genetic or innate propensities (nature). They can even override the innate factors; aggressive strains of mice and dogs can be trained early in life to inhibit these reactions, both offensive and defensive, through socialization, that is, affection training and attachment, or inhibitory training, i.e., discipline.

This "nurture" aspect of aggression casts doubt on Lorenz's thesis and gives some hope against the supporters of the "nature" or innate view. If aggression were a totally inborn drive, then little could be done to control it; early training and socialization would be ineffectual, but this is far from the truth. In fact, both dogs and people often have such strong social inhibitions against fighting that considerable training and provocation through indoctrination and propaganda in man is required.*

An understanding of the factors that trigger reactions of aggression is important in its control, although such knowledge could and has been used to make dogs fight and men wage war. Priva-

---

* Interestingly, the behaviour of submission/surrender in dog and man normally cuts off the aggressor's attack, but in the "push-button war"—killing at a distance—such natural inhibitory mechanisms break down. Thus, coupled with the programmed propaganda that the enemy are something less than human, a man has no inhibitions about dropping napalm on women and children.

Photo: Winnipeg Sunday News Magazine
Admiring their "catch," airplane hunters hold annual wolf shoot: a
"sport" they obviously enjoy.

tion or frustration of basic needs—food, territory, personal rights and freedom—experienced collectively as a shared crisis, either real or exaggerated by inflammatory warlords or politicians, may unify a people for war. Similarly, a hungry or sexually frustrated animal is more likely to fight. Only a generation ago educators thought that raising children with minimal frustration would reduce aggressivity in adulthood. How wrong they were in indulging a child's every whim; such children never developed adequate coping strategies for the frustrations they would eventually encounter as adults in the "real world."

Fear, rather than frustration, may trigger defensive aggression. The natural suspicion and fear of strangers xenophobia has tradi- The natural suspicion and fear of strangers (xenophobia) has traditionally been used by leaders to bring the populace to arms against others of a different race or culture. Defensive aggression, justified by paranoid projections, quickly turns into offensive aggression, as exemplified by Hitler's genocidal programs against Jews.

As a man can be conditioned, indoctrinated, and sensitized to aggress against his own kind, he also has the capacity to learn to *control* aggressive reactions. We cannot conclude, therefore, that basic human nature is innately aggressive, although the ability to react aggressively is clearly inborn. No social animal has an inborn tendency to aggress against its own kind, since such programming would be detrimental to the survival and continuation of the species. Through natural and social selection various mechanisms to rein in aggression and to prevent severe injury have evolved in many species, e.g., the ritualized wrestling of snakes who do not use their venom on each other or the inhibited muzzle-biting of wolves and their displays of submission to the pack leader. Such natural controls break down in both man and animal, however, when basic needs are frustrated; and in man in the face of xenophobia and political indoctrination. The environment —the social/political milieu—is to blame in man; it is his *human nurture,* not human nature, that is at fault. Once we accept the basic goodness of humankind and reinforce rather than belittle that intrinsic goodness, and also focus our attention on the real causes of aggression, then we may be able to work constructively for peace. No man or nation wants war unless there is want, frustration, paranoia, or motives of power and greed, or the need to impose one's values and political ideology on others in order to control and exploit them (often under the guise of altruism). There are alternatives to war and to the fulfillment of personal and national want alike. We have evolved a science and technology of war, but as yet we have not developed to the same degree the mechanisms whereby we may bring about and maintain peace. The solutions for peace rest in the causes of war, not within the hearts of men but in the illusory world man has fabricated and which he can also change.

Since there is no primary drive or need to aggress, one must look beneath the overtly aggressive behaviour for an underlying cause. There is a "law of opposites" with people—the more aggressive, assertive, or pushy they may seem, the more they are insecure and uncertain or hurt deep within themselves. On the surface is the compensation—the ego's defenses. Similarly, pain or fear may underlie aggressive reaction in both animals and people, who may therefore be easily misjudged if not fully understood. Another example of such compensation is the man who tries to be perfect, like the psychiatrist who fears failure (the suicide of a single patient) and, being aware of his limitations, overcompensates. Ultimately he may succeed in convincing himself that he is, in fact, perfect, and megalomania develops—from an ego defense against inferiority or fear of failure. The "law of opposites" is indeed a factor that causes much confusion in understanding human behaviour, especially when the observer gets hooked by someone's belligerent or know-it-all façade.

Beneath the façade of the alcoholic, sociopath, madman, and murderer lies suffering. With understanding one can "turn the other cheek," but we must be prepared to defend ourselves (and them, also) from themselves, rather than condemn them. With understanding no man will fall into the ignorance of judging others, for with understanding comes help in forgiveness. Remember, too, we tend to judge and condemn in others those qualities we like least in ourselves.

And so many of us condemn the hunter; even Thoreau wrote that every man must mature through the immature phase of being a hunter and eventually lay down his gun. Since it is the male ego that is so deeply ingrained with the hunting instinct inherited from our forefathers, we must consider some other aspects of such an immature ego or primitive psychological set.

Part of the creative genius of *Homo sapiens* is his ability to see *into* the things around him, to convert them to his own uses, and to use them to satisfy his many needs. A rock may be shaped into a flint; a deer represents potential food and clothing and fishing lines made from skin and sinews; a tree, timber for a house; a river, a source of hydroelectric energy; a wilderness of shale, energy for our cities. As man evolves and explores the world around him, he discovers ever more things to satisfy and support society and technology's energy-consuming creations.

The world is seen in terms of one's own *needs,* and a new discovery, a new source of energy, or a faster or more productive machine is a mark of progress. The male ego is fed by values supporting growth, progress, and exploration. The individual takes pride in accomplishment and a warm aura of status at success, as did the ancestral hunter who first used a flint-headed spear to provide meat for his family.

The tragic flaw in human perception, though, is that modern man does not really *see* the world as it is, but only in terms of how it can satisfy needs. "See me for what I am, not as you wish to use me," is the cry of women's lib. It could also be the cry of wilderness, of wolves, of deer, rivers, and trees.

A man who really *sees* a woman for what she is and vice versa may truly experience love, that oneness which religion has failed to give most of us and which, in its absence, creates the endless searching and restlessness of hollow people. People who desperately seek alternative fulfillment in temporary satisfaction in the countless diversions of both work and play in our culture find at best only fleeting happiness.

Nothing is real in such a world. A man who sees the wilderness, wolves, deer, rivers, and trees for what they are—separate from his own needs and the values he foists on them—finds his world has become more real. He will experience that oneness with things that will make him think twice before felling an ancient tree, home to millions of generations of birds, insects, and small animals, in order to clear a road or provide lumber for a house. He will *seek alternatives,* as must the two nations which still kill whales—Russia and Japan. In thinking twice he is clearing his eyes and beginning to *see* at last—he sees the tree, like the woman, not in terms of how he may use or exploit it. He sees and appreciates the thing for itself.

Seeing an eagle, a puma, a wolf, or a whale as the thing in itself, no man could kill it without first questioning his own motivations. In seeing, such a man has matured at last beyond the primitive ego that feels pride and status in hunting and killing rival hunters. He has matured by establishing a new connection in his brain and by breaking an old one inherited from his fore-fathers. The new connection gives him a greater awareness that is the key to understanding life for what it is, and others for what they are. The old connection tied him to the world, where the world of nature, the biosphere, is merely an extension of himself, an "egosphere" if you wish. Once broken, he becomes a free man, no longer controlled by or imposing his needs, values, and rights on others, be they wolves, women, or other men. Other people—wolves and indeed all living things—are suddenly seen to have rights and intrinsic values. Their needs can now be understood at last, and are no longer felt as a threat to the fulfillment of one's own.

Man the hunter may then become a *life hunter,* free now to seek the richer things in life based on relationship and kinship. He no longer destroys without knowing, and he may look for alternatives to felling an old tree or to hunting and trapping wild animals for sport, enjoyment, financial gain, or other ego satis-factions.

Few of us hunt for food today, and if everyone did, there would soon be nothing left in our forests. Ecologically speaking, when man began to domesticate plants and animals ten thousand years ago and his population began to explode, the hunting way of life became neither economically nor ecologically realistic.

Without our domestic plants and animals today, we would indeed starve. The fact that people still hunt today in order to satisfy an ancient ritual must be seen in a broader ecological context. In order to satisfy such needs, game—be it deer, partridge, quail, or even imported game from Africa—has to be carefully managed and often artificially propagated. Natural predators—wolves cougars, bobcats, and even foxes—would compete with the hunter for such varied game, and the old practice of management involved extermination of such rival hunters. Hunters know today, however, that where there are wolves, the deer are healthier. They no longer blame the wolf for decline in deer populations since the mismanagement of forests where there is no controlled burning is, instead, often the cause. Since the deer have no browse to eat in a forest of prime timber, they starve to death.

The preservationist is as misguided in his or her notion of "hands off nature" as is the hunter who shoots a cougar for sport. The hunter may contribute to the destruction of an ecosystem by killing off key predators who regulate the population of grass-eating mammals. The preservationist may ring the bell of doom on an ecosystem that is not wilderness but that is out of balance (with few predators) and needs managing or that is all prime timber. Even Smokey the Bear isn't too cool today—forest fires are an essential part of forest ecology and management!

I must address the hunter who goes into an area to bag grouse or deer that have been managed for him. He is *part of that ecosystem,* and without him overpopulation, overgrazing, and crowding stress would soon cause a rapid die-off of his target species. In parts of Africa today the elephant is too abundant and is destroying the habitat. Hundreds must be killed. Why? Because native hunting of elephants is banned, whereas for thousands of years the black hunter was part of that ecosystem, like the wolf hunting the deer on our own continent.

Is it fair, in terms of animal rights—of seeing and appreciating the thing for itself—for modern man to compete for game with fox, coyote, wolf, or cougar? Would it not be a tremendous step forward to reintroduce, in areas well buffered from farmland (where there are cattle and sheep), some of these larger predators?

Ecologically speaking, they would be ideal game managers. And in terms of rights surely man, who has domestic animals and plants and oceans to give him all the food he needs, has neither need nor right to compete with them.

A man hunting in an area where deer or other game are managed on his behalf is part of such an ecosystem, artificial as it is. But I would like him to reflect on what I have said. Mightn't he indeed take greater pleasure in shooting a deer many times with a *camera* and in discovering some of the secrets of animal behaviour in a natural ecosystem, rather than one managed artificially for his enjoyment, which, after all, is no more than a wild game ranch?

What of the hunter who goes into relatively unmanaged wilderness? When such a man begins to see, he will exchange his gun for a camera. Why should any man who knows a bear, a wolf, or a cougar for what it is even *contemplate* killing it for sport?

Yes, it is the overriding motive of conquest that is the stamp of modern man, as it was of our primitive hunter ancestors. For similiar ego reasons man will strive to conquer cougar, wolf, deer, women, oceans, mountains, new continents—even outer space. So preoccupied with such outer diversions, we have hardly begun to explore the "inner space" of ourselves. The greatest conquest for man is the "inner space" of his being.

It is a difficult journey when you feel judged or threatened, and I hope that you who carry guns have not felt this from me. After all, we are brothers. I, too, love all that is natural and wild, but unlike you, I no longer kill for sport. I feed my family only from the oceans and from the fields of our farmers whose forefathers took that land from wild animals and plants, and who manage it for us today. Once a man can see a tree, a coyote, or his fellow, and value the other for what it or he or she is, his world becomes profoundly different. He will rediscover the brotherhood of humanity and foster it in others and in his children. Kinship with nature, which many hunters have, is the key to this awareness. No man can look inward, however, when he is regarding the world through the sights of a gun.

8

Man, Progress, and Ecology

The agriculturist forgets that his livestock may cause epidemic diseases in wild herbivores, although he is aware that the wild animals may serve as a reservoir of disease to infect his own stock. The extinction of wild herbivores means little, except perhaps that there will be more food for domestic stock. We forget that man replaces many of the larger carnivores with himself, the wild herbivores with his own stock, and wild plants with his own high-producing hybrids. This replacement of the natural flora and fauna with those of an artificial ecosystem would seem vital in order to meet the world's growing food demands, but is it in fact the most efficient and productive way? Are there other alternatives? The modern farm industry is analogous to the automated mass production factory, producing the same items on the assembly line. Such specialization—beef or pork from one farm factory, corn or wheat from another—may appear the most efficient method of production, but it can lead to overspecialization that has many self-limiting elements.

Overproduction can bring an unusable surplus. Worse, the system is not flexible: All the eggs are in one basket in a monolithic system that may be wiped out by fungal blight or epidemic disease. A better and more flexible, self-contained system of farming is the "mixed" method, best exemplified by the Norfolk crop rotation system. A more complex system like this has the advantages not only of flexibility but of self-support, where, for example, grazing beef cattle enrich the fields with their manure for root or cereal crops, and these provide bedding for the animals in the winter. Millions of tons of valuable manure are wasted in beef lots today, and the straw from our wheat fields, a valuable commodity, is wasted, too. A good cost analysis may show that the specialized monolithic farming of all corn or all beef, for example, may give more profit and is less work than a mixed system. But a mixed system with its intrinsic diversity may be far more productive in the long run, perhaps over a period of one or two hundred years or more.

We are learning today what specialized farming does to the land. For example, with cereal farming no nitrogen-fixing legumes are ever grown nor cattle grazed to manure the land. Artificial fertilizers are instead dumped by the ton on land that is becoming soured and impoverished. We must learn from nature and model our artificial ecosystems after those of the biosphere (see figure, next page) The least diverse natural ecosystems, like the arctic tundra, are the most fragile. With diversity and intrinsic complexity there is flexibility, a wide safety margin (vis-à-vis disease, blight, or overproduction), and a better use of energy resources by self-containment. This aspect, as exemplified by the plant-animal food chain in nature, should be replicated in our farming practices if we hope to continue to feed the world and not destroy it and ourselves in the process.

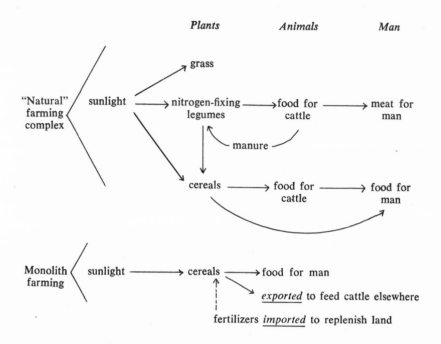

In wanting more we produce more, and also in fulfilling our dreams of progress and growth we deplete the biosphere of its natural resources. Modern man is in dire need of a new ethic—a new value system—in order to be "needless" in the ego-transcending sense. The cancerous growth of both the human population and our energy-consuming artifacts alike must be controlled; the long-term consequences of man having stepped out of the biosphere, out of the direct and directing influences of natural selection and regulation, must be recognized. Before this great evolutionary step ten thousand years ago, man was essentially still part of the Garden of Eden. Man was as an animal, under more direct influence of the forces of nature. But now he is more under self-control and must assume the full responsibilities for a dilemma that could destroy him or lead to the fulfillment of all our dreams and potentials.

Man is becoming supra-tribal, and a global conscience and consciousness can flower once there is unity in terms of goals and resources alike. No nation can be allowed to assume power and control over others. Instead, domination by one must be replaced by support and ecologically sensible aid from all. Otherwise even the most advanced societies will flounder because there is only *one world* and because what happens in one country now has global ecological as well as political ramifications, as exemplified today by the famines of the east and the Arab oil crisis. We must all assume full responsibility for the consequences of our actions and inaction alike. One cardinal sign of eco-cancer is "more," e.g., building a dam to produce more power for consumption. *Little is better and more is worse than nothing at all.**

There are many of us with a wide range of talents, and it is fortunate that we can create useful niches or roles in a synthetic ecosystem of increasing complexity that develops naturally as a society industrializes. With increasing specialization and complexity a web of interdependence for materials and products is elaborated. Much like a tropical rain forest (a climax ecology), an advanced industrialized society has many interdependent roles/niches. But the forest needs the sun, its foundation, and for the Western world this is fossil fuel. The wolf needs the deer; the salesman, a buyer; the bird, twigs for its nest; the builder, concrete and metal. But unlike man, no animal produces in order to create a surplus. *The profit motive of the materialistic system is self-destructive because it insures a constant spiralling of production costs and consumption prices.* This is where, unlike the rain forest, the man-made eco-complex breaks down (self-regulating negative feedback is lacking).

If wolves had to kill more deer in order to live—to support an artificially created want—the deer would have to breed more, which might be possible if the grass could be persuaded to produce more. But there is only one sun—ultimately a finite energy source from which a limited surplus may be reaped. Man can and does make the grass produce more, but he cannot make another sun to meet the demands of increasing energy requirements.

If the production-consumption cancer were stopped today and

---

* For an excellent economic treatise on this new ethic, see *Small Is Beautiful* by E. F. Schumacher, Harper & Row, 1974.

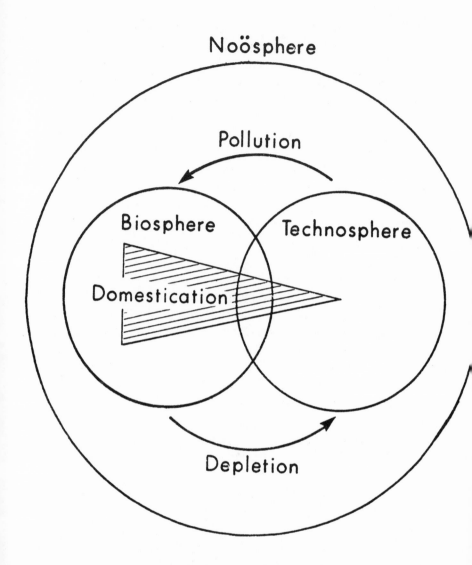

Schema of the destructive effects of the technosphere on the bio-sphere; the former must become self-sustaining and alternative energy sources be sought, together with population/pollution and energy consumption control. Eco-crisis may unify us in collective global action—the noösphere of a truly global (rather than tribal or national) humanity.

population growth was controlled, we could work with some predictable goals, rather than make projections of what the world's "needs" (fuel and energy) will be in twenty years' time. We have hardly begun to apply our technology toward increasing the "bio-efficiency" of raising food (hydroponics) and of harnessing solar energy. Using atomic energy as a stopgap, as we now use fossil fuels, would only be temporary, and the health and "eco-hazards" many times greater. Let our success in more intensive, self-contained agriculture and more direct usage of solar energy (rather than indirectly through fossil fuels) not lead us into a second cancerous era of abundance and technological production/consumption growth.

Consider the socio-ecology of the cow, dog, and beggars of India's cities. Even high in the caste system people are not without unsatisfied needs—hunger for bread, security, power, sex, love, knowledge, and spirituality at all levels. Happiness is transient reinforcement, momentary fulfillment before the same hunger or the hunger at the next level appears. (Beggars reach to me; those with bread reach to the guru—to whom does the guru reach?) There seems no end to human suffering and want.

Humanitarian "good will" can also disrupt the natural balance of things. For example, providing medicine and food to an "underdeveloped" country, without backing it up with agricultural reforms and birth control, will only aggravate the population crisis and postpone the inevitable suffering of famine and disease. Similarly, we may help "develop" a primitive society such as a tribe of South American Indians. When "discovered," they live simply, their population in balance with the carrying capacity of their natural ecosystem. We teach them to develop an artificial ecosystem so that they may produce more and have more. We give them our values—progress, production, and profit. They soon set up ecological disequilibriums, clearing vast areas of forest, destroying natural habitats. With more food there are more children and more children need more food. Raw materials or products are produced as a rudimentary technology evolves.

They produce more so that they may have more, and in order to have even more, they must produce *still* more. Having little is unsatisfactory, and greed, status, and power appear. Needs are eventually created so that people will want unessential items, indeed so that they cannot "live" (or enjoy life) without them. A symbolic example is that of a new Guinea headhunter with spear in one hand and a transistor radio in the other. The cancer of progress has been sown in their minds. No one can ever have everything, or even enough of anything. So there springs a constant unrest, a neurotic yearning for more. In truth, the man who has nothing and desires nothing has all.

Nothing that happens is bad, unless we do not learn from it. There is neither right nor wrong, but a man is at fault if he judges others or is not *aware* of the sources and consequences of his own actions and does not assume reponsibility for them. He who judges others must expect others to judge him. In the unitive world of metavalues differences are accepted, and since people are aware of themselves, there is no judgment, but only evaluation which is without condemnation and which gives one the freedom to accept or reject *without* judgment. ("I choose to disagree with him," rather than "He's a fool because he can't see it my way," or "If he was aware of and responsible for his choice of action, what he did I must accept, even though I don't agree," rather than "What he did was wrong.") If I don't feel okay about someone else's actions or values, I must resolve this by finding out if that person was aware and responsible at the time he acted. This way I come closer to him. I learn and do not cut him and myself off in judgment or condemnation.

Conservation is consciousness-raising in action. It is a reaffirmation of the man/nature unity. We discover unity in rational values and ethically responsible actions. Man has been separated from nature by his beliefs and actions (culture), as his mind is separated from his body. Today man is rediscovering more of his own nature (as exemplified by books such as *Naked Ape* and the human potential movement) and of nature per se (the post-Thoreau renaissance in ecological, holistic Zen and Taoistic philosophies). Unity of man/nature and mind/body will reduce the void between man and man, man and animal, and man and God —animal, man, and God representing the three stages of awareness in the evolution of consciousness.

A holistic view of man in the world and the world within man is what is needed. It will reveal the continuity between animal and man in terms of needs, feelings (emotion), bonds of affection, group pressures and bonds of belonging, and also in terms of conformity and the conflict between self and others' needs and wants.

Awareness of this and of man's ultimate responsibility for his own destiny places him in the position of a god. He is free to develop—to evolve under his own direction—but he is *not* free to be irresponsible, since this new awareness involves even greater responsibility than ever before. It is difficult for a man to discover himself without exploring the world around him, and nature can be the key to such self-discovery. Until man learns again to live at one with nature, he will never be at one with himself. The imprint to date of man on nature clearly reveals the sickness as well as the infinite potential of his being. Progress is endless, but we forget that nature's resources are finite—this is the reality our dreamers forget. Progressive growth without awareness of consequences is cancer on a global scale, and we must all assume responsibility for our own and others' actions since, like it or not, we *are* involved and there is nowhere else to go.

9

Creation, Conservation, and the Future of Man

Man is a product of creation, of evolution. He was part of a process that shaped the earth, all life forms, and our minds alike. Now he is reshaping the earth, altering all life forms (plant and animal), which are being either domesticated or managed and conserved in the natural or seminatural wild state. Man, therefore, a product of creation, is now a creator. The creative process has actualized itself and has been internalized in human consciousness and is externalized or expressed in creative and innovative actions and devices, first in agriculture and later in technology. Man is then both process and processor, creation and creator, both animal and God—or, in the religious vernacular, God is incarnate in man, or at least potentially so. In other words, nature gains ultimate expression, in consciousness, through man.

The potential and resources of the original creative process are infinite, relative to the potential and resources available to man. Perhaps not, though. The actualization of potentials, synthesis and integration of new potentiality, and efficient utilization of material resources are surely a function of the degree of individual and collective (cultural) consciousness. For example, the conceptualizations of Leonardo da Vinci were generations ahead of their time—ahead of the consensus values of his society, whose needs, conservatism-conformity, and limited awareness put many of his brilliant blueprints out of its reach. Nor were the resources always available to realize some of his "far-out" inventions. Leonardo, like many, was in the right place at the wrong time.

Once the rate of exchange or interchange between mind potentialities and environmental and sociocultural potentials slows down, then the creative process within a culture is arrested. Unless catalyzed by a farsighted genius or innovator, stability leads to decay—the creative process atrophies and dies—as in the rise and fall of civilizations. This pattern surely mirrors the original creative process itself—the rise and fall of predominant ecosystems and flora and fauna, many of which are now extinct or exist in modified form as "primitive" living fossils. Many existing cultures, values, rituals, and ways of thinking today are analogous to such contemporary biological anachronisms.

One reason for the slowing down of the creative/evolutionary process is overspecialization, so that new ecological niches or environmental and sociocultural potential cannot be exploited. This is true of plant, animal, man, and civilization alike. Monolithic civilizations are doomed. Diversity, flexibility, and the renaissance view must counterbalance the acquisition of specialized skills, roles, and ways of thinking: The open syntonic system versus the stable but entropic closed system. (Entropy is also caused by biological or cultural conservatism that stabilizes the evolutionary/creative process but that can also destroy it.)

Suppose, in contrast, that the creative process breaks loose from such balancing restraints, i.e., more Yang than Yin—Tao is destroyed. Spurned by national values maintaining that all growth and change is progress, the result would be catastrophe: At the biological level a population explosion and crash, or a cosmic conflagration. We see such parallels in our technocratic society today—the cancerous growth of energy-consuming needs and artifacts; pollution and overexploitation of the biosphere; future shock among men and women, emotional and social inability of people to adapt to information overload, and a continuously accelerating rate of change.

Man, product of creation and now creator himself, must assume full global socioecological responsibility for his actions and inaction. The Tao must be restored, as well as the balance of Yin and Yang. To slow down "progress," to reduce production consumption, is not a backward step—it is an essential one toward restoration of balance. Society and its economy will have to be restructured, and some institutions, occupations, and values will undergo extinction much as the dinosaurs before them. This is a minor catastrophe compared to the predictable conflagration and disintegration that is inevitable if the direction of development continues. A change in consciousness is all that is required, both at the level of the individual and of the collective consensus of society.

Human *beings* are good: It is human *doings* that are bad, creating the monster of global technocracy—a materialistic, exploitative interdependency, where love, brotherhood, and humane ethics are neither used, needed, valued, or encouraged. Culture disintegrates as nation states are unified or, rather, drawn together by the growing tentacles of the technosphere—not into true unity but rather into a loss of original purpose and identity in the shared values of transcultural *materialism*. This monster causes spiritual, interpersonal, and ecological disruption and pollution. If we can free our ego-involvement and dependence upon it and ally our essence and being with the fundamental essence and being of all things, then the monster will destroy itself. Without this breaking away, it will destroy its creator, mankind, who is caught in the worship and support of his creations.

I place so much emphasis on human values because these are determined by national and international consensus, which in turn determine our priorities and actions. Our attachment, dependence, and intimate knowledge of the physical/material world of our bodies, machines, and ecosystems is an egocentric existential "cop-out," if all is not integrated in space/time. Our endeavors and awareness must be seen in a global/evolutionary perspective. We inherit the potential of our forefathers, and their unfinished business is our Karma. We must each strive in our lifetimes to clear this Karmic burden and work toward our own self-actualization* in order to lighten the burden and clear the way for our children and their children's children.

We must ask what all this is worth—all that we do—in relation to human evolution and the welfare of the planet as a whole. Egocentric values and irrational moral standards are no basis for adequate evaluation. So much of our knowledge and resources alike are misused in shortsighted gratification of personal and national needs. A more holistic world view with new values and symbols is urgently needed to give human life a sense of continuity, purpose, and direction. Life is essentially personal, but it becomes a transpersonal experience of far greater significance and potential fulfillment once this world view is achieved. Then, through the totality of self as part of the creative process, the transient, mortal things of this life and of this civilization take on new dimensions. One then participates selflessly, and with a sense of commitment that comes with the freedom to be responsible, in the process of living and evolving. Man then becomes eternal—part of a universal whole. In his own lifetime and for succeeding generations, consciousness-raising and spiritual unfoldment transform existence. Reverence for life and all living things determines our thinking and being.† This is not for our generation, or perhaps for our civilization, since we are only a link in the continuum. This is the fundamental truth of our mortal existence, and it is the only foundation on which all purpose, direction, and human striving should be based.

---

* Or dharma fulfillment.
† Wherein lies our dharma fulfillment.

10

Some Issues and
Actions in Conservation

Man's place in nature is seen by some in a pacifist framework in which man lets nature alone and both live at peace. This idealized view of the preservationist is unreal, since there is no part of this earth that is not affected by some consequence of man's action upon the biosphere. Oceans are polluted, and the rains that fall where no man has ever walked carry industrial wastes. Even the upper atmosphere is polluted, and the protective ozone layer that filters dangerous ultraviolet light may ultimately be destroyed.

It is vital for man's own health and for the integrity of the biosphere that he monitor every action and interaction. For some this sounds like management, but in reality the "hands-off" policy of the preservationist would be suicidal. Rather than "management," tainted with the raising and management of species and ecosystems solely for human use, the term "stewardship" is more appropriate. Implicit in stewardship is action (rather than pacifist, Zenlike inaction) and reverence for all life. As Albert Schweitzer observed, "An ethics that does not consider our relation to the world of creatures is incomplete. The struggle against inhumanity must be waged wholly and continually. We must

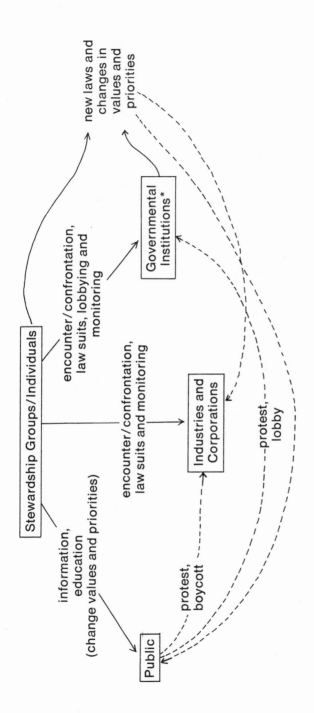

*Find the more liberal individuals who are willing to "live danger-ously" in a bureaucracy. Responsible stewards must have office at local, state and federal levels.

reach the stage at which killing for sport will be felt as a disgrace to our civilization."

But advertising and promotion of sport and luxury, unessential trophy hunting, and the wearing of wild-caught furs,* are only three value systems that must be changed. There are other vogue enthusiasms that will be even more difficult to oppose since they ramify more widely and more deeply into the very fabric of our culture. Consider this year's misplaced priorities on:

1) recreational rights that allow people to disturb, pollute, and destroy habitats with snowmobiles, speed boats on inland lakes, and motorcycles that plough up deserts and disturb the sanctity of mountain wilderness; and also on

2) multiple land use, pleasing everyone and meeting everyone's needs democratically—a utopian dream that satisfies only a few and is potentially destructive. Add to this the *modification and/or destruction of natural ecosystems* to create recreational facilities (e.g., the rash of artificial lakes) reflecting primarily financial interests and privileged minority enjoyment. And bear in mind also the habitat destruction provoked by the national need for food and natural resources (fossil fuels). As the need for more energy spirals with a growing world population and a spreading technology, global ecocide seems inevitable.

At home priorities governing the use of public land may be awarded to mining or drilling companies to meet national needs. Conservationists and preservationists alike may then be branded traitors. A new ethic governing the values of growth and progress of production and energy consumption is vitally needed. "Little is beautiful; big is ugly, not better." Unlimited growth in technology and the human population alike are two forms of global cancer that are synergistic and that can only be inhibited by a drastic change in human values, which in turn will cause a change in our needs and priorities.

---

* Placing some furbearers on the endangered species list has lead to even greater depredations on other nonendangered furbearers like bobcat and lynx. The "endangered" list is a compromise between hunter and conservationist. Nothing today can be compromised. There can be no half measures in the humane ethic.

Finally, *direct competition* with another species for some natural resource or food source brings up the perennial issue of animal versus human rights. With an ethic of reverence for all life, a man only kills out of necessity and looks first for alternatives, rather than engaging in habitual destruction. Such an ethic is needed today in the sheep ranching industry, where poisoning of renegade coyotes entails indiscriminate slaughter of all wildlife. But *who* cried out when all the wild plants were destroyed for the sake of corn and wheat, and harmless butterflies and other insects, birds, and mammals of the original prairie ecosystem were eliminated for national profit a few years ago? And is destruction now warranted in the face of national need and global starvation? What conservationists could argue against such destruction in order to save a starving village in India? What if his own children were starving? How can we discriminate between human and nonhuman rights and still uphold the ethic of reverence for all life in the face of dire human need? If we destroy knowingly and seek other alternatives like birth control, voluntary sterilization, and abortion, hydroponics and aquaculture, does our guilt diminish?

The earth is going through a profound climatic change. Another ice age is predicted, and the question of survival in the face of drought and famine and other more devastating and unpredictable future catastrophes will be a major concern of future generations. Will man return to the ethic of "kill or be killed." Must the last tiger die so that one family may eat for one more week?

It is hoped humanity may discover unity under such crises, and the value of each life will be so magnified through individual suffering that a true spirituality may emerge and be expressed in a reverence for all life. In times of crisis, suffering, and destruction, the best and the worst qualities of humanity are clear. We must begin today to foster the former, not as an escape from reality but as the only way to meet the inevitable reality of the crisis to come.

Today we can all begin by finding unity through common goals and accepting differences in philosophy, whether it be between conservation organizations or nations. In conservation we must be alert to the possibility that special interest groups (e.g. sport/ hunting or mining) may gain a monopoly control over some part of the biosphere. It is vital at local, state, and national levels for there to be representation of different values, needs, and priorities. Monolithic organizations are not only unconstitutional; they are potentially destructive and blatantly ignore a prime human resource—diversity of opinion, interest, and knowledge.

The conservationist can participate significantly at many interphases in the complex machinery of our society. He can do more than carry a placard in front of the White House, deploring the President's ignorance in wearing a wolf fur coat.* The fact that he wore it is more potent and self-evident truth than a whole line of demonstrators. There are many more effective options than fruitless protest for the conservationist or, as I would like to rename such people, stewards of the earth. They need have no special credentials or knowledge (although some helps), only a commitment to life and to the highest ethic of reverence for all life. If a man must destroy and kill, let him do so in full conscience and awareness; otherwise his own death will also be in ignorance, and the value and purpose of his life will lack meaning.

I have summarized in a simplified information-theory format (See Figure 1), where stewardship may be effectively undertaken in the struggle against inhumane values and the destructive forces around us. The effort to raise the consciousness of our fellow men and women so that we may all attain a more complete fulfillment in life is an obligation we have not only to our children, but to all life, because we *are* human. If we abdicate or violate this responsibility, we are something less than man, and in so doing we make a mockery of the whole process of evolution and of the purpose of our own existence on this small planet.

One of the first things that strikes a European visitor to the United States is the incredible mobility of people. Small families stay in one place for two or three years and then move on. This is partly a consequence of the demands of a job market in which

---

* Which is now apparently in mothballs.

a man must either move to better himself or in which he works for a company with a policy of transferring their personnel every few years. What are the social implications? To an outsider, it seems a *neurotic* kind of social mobility. A stranger visits one town after another—especially in the Midwest—and is amazed at the similarity of the layout. The terrain is similar; he can count on a gasoline station or a fast food stand on every corner, and the block system, designed not in the European radial style, but more in a linear grid fashion, is uniform, if not monotonous. Certainly a person moving into such an area from a similar one should be able to adapt very easily. Perhaps, too, such mobile people in moving into a new place that is virtually a mirror image of the place where they were born and raised, or where they have previously lived for a few years, experience no real homesickness— just a transient sense of loss of friends that, hopefully, will soon be dispelled as they acquire new ones.

To be attached to old trees and old buildings, unusual configurations of streets, steep hillsides, and so on, is all part of a man's experience of the spirit of place. Deprived of the familiar, he suffers the syndrome known as homesickness, a syndrome common to many cultures. In animals this is referred to as philopatry, or "locality imprinting." Essentially it is an emotional attachment to one's place of birth or homeland. Now a person born and raised in an anonymous or unremarkable locale is less likely to experience this sort of homesickness (although he may miss his immediate relatives), and so the suburban uniformity we see stretching across the United States must certainly help people to be increasingly and comfortably mobile. Very probably it renders it easier to tear up roots and move on. But in spite of this, the *constant* uprooting must have some significant social and emotional consequences.

Are such modern, mobile families less likely to set up close, enduring friendships? It would seem pointless if they are to move after only a short stay in a particular place. All this may be very well in the pursuit of happiness through increased affluence— the main motive for moving—but what about man's social and

Suburban developments create false unity through uniformity, and replace anything natural with expedient symmetry and convenient concrete.

Two urban ecologies—"primitive ruralized" Madras, with the litter of progress on the pavements, and industrialized Los Angeles, with automobile and other pollutants in the air.

biological needs? One of his basic needs is to belong to a group, a tribe, an extended family—*but he has none*. He has his wife and a few children and pets, and nothing else. His immediate relatives are perhaps thousands of miles away. He feels isolated, lonely. No longer do we have the extended nuclear family and clan with supportive relatives close at hand. No longer do we have a tribe and rarely do we have a community in the real sense of the word. Many young people today, sensing this lack, are moving into urban areas and helping organize neighborhood blocks. Others have been setting up and living in urban and rural communes.

Consider a mobile society made up of family units with little allegiance to a given area and, of course, equally little interest in its progress, design, and ecology, or in the well-being of those other people who will remain there after the mobile unit has gone on. As a consequence, they have very little local political involvement. They are at once uncommitted and alienated. For the corporate-controllers this is perhaps the ideal situation—a populace that really couldn't care less about local government. In this way it is very easy to manipulate the masses, who are constantly mobile and have little interest in anything local or regional. The construction of a dam, draining of a swamp, or destruction of a forest, has little significance to transients.

Yet one can identify, as a result of this almost neurotic mobility, intense feelings of insecurity and of loneliness. There is a lack of permanence in these peoples' physical as well as emotional environment and in relationships with nature and other men and women alike.

In primitive hunter-gatherer societies, where one individual went, the whole group went. There was a solid sense of community. In the few remaining farming communities in this country and in the small rural towns we have a stronger sense of community, and it is here that we find some political strength. Because this regional political power only exists in less mobile minority groups of our society—groups representing but a small segment of the populace—we have grounds for a pessimistic view of the future, both politically and ecologically. What is the remedy? And how can we catalyze in the majority of Americans living in the isolated dream world of suburbia (the urban dormitories) a sense of commitment, both spiritually and materially, to the land, to their natural heritage, as well as to each other?

Within hunting-gathering societies there was also a mixture within the group of ages and roles. Consequently, the child growing up got a great deal of enrichment from older people and from people who assumed different roles—as hunter, musician, storyteller, and so on—widening the child's experience of the world through communicating their own. In modern society there is, effectively, impoverishment in the sense of children meeting people who have different societal roles. People of the same profession tend to band together. And the age segregation in modern Western society, in which old people are no longer part of the extended nuclear family but live in retirement condominiums, nursing homes, or alone in welfare tenements, is perhaps more serious than our professional and race/class segregations.

In essence, therefore, the more society becomes stratified into roles and divided up in terms of age (and I should remind you that we now advertise community settlements for the unmarried "swinging singles" as well as retirement villages for "senior citizens"), the more we limit the enrichment that comes of meeting people of different ages and points of view. The sense of isolation, of loneliness, of alienation, and of emptiness in life is inevitably intensified. Modern society must return again to a concept of geographic stability—stability of social relationships; return again to valuing the aged for the gift of experience they can give to young children and to society in general. Revising major life priorities entails looking at one's own personal needs and identifying precisely where and why they are not being met by society or by the life-style one has adopted. I have no intention of attempting to convince the man who moves his family every two or three years in quest of happiness through a fat paycheck to look at his needs and to find, in fact, that his life is relatively empty so far as nonmaterial enrichment is concerned— in being close to people and in being involved in community and conservation activities, both political and social. Nor will I pre-

sume to provide answers for the social psychologist or the economist. All that I can offer are some perceptions of society as I
see it—first, as an involved member, and second, as a researcher
into human and animal behaviour.

One of the dilemmas of the human condition is that man is
both part of, yet apart from, nature. He seeks unity of his primitive essence with nature. Even the most sophisticated of technological men yearn for it. The more advanced, the more isolated,
or the more individuated he becomes, the greater the sense of
aloneness, and the greater the need for integration—for group
identification, for group involvement—and for oneness with nature. The weekend in the country or that camping vacation becomes a meaningful and much needed experience, not simply an
escape from the hustle and bustle of workaday life. It is a time
when one can be at ease with nature, and perhaps for a moment
transcend and feel oneness with something greater than oneself,
greater than man has been able to manufacture for himself.
Modern youth is in awe of and envies the "primitives" like the
American Indians, who have a religion and philosophy that make
a person feel at one with the world and at peace—content with
his bridges of magic, myth, and music, rather than with the artifacts of consumerism. These bridges are the bridges science has
not built for us, but which the primitive can cross to find powers
of ecstasy and worlds beyond the trivial and transient world of
materialism we have made for ourselves.

When man begins to alter his environment through his technology, he may lag behind in adapting himself to the changes
he has brought about with his own skills. We see man in his technological world, or *technosphere,* becoming at one with the system he has created: He is controlled by the social machine. His
identity dissolves into a collective, corporate one. He does not see
himself as at once an individual and a part of the continuum. Instead, he has *security:* All is defined on an IBM card owned by
the system which is his surrogate mother, a facsimile of the continuum. He has adapted, done the "normal," acceptable thing. But
we must question the normality and reality of this state when he
feels that he no longer has any identity. There is a growing ten-

sion because of the need for a more personalized and actualizing state, and a corollary conflict because security seems to be a safe position to be in and the "void" is unknown. With "technoinvolution," the global spread of technology which brings remote corners of the world together, there is a feeling of interdependence and a unity, but it is a false unity. By adapting to the technological environment—and when I say adapting, I imply total immersion and loss of individuality—a man becomes a culturally different subspecies, *Homo technos.* He is no longer part of the biosphere. He is part of a self-made, artificial environment we might call an "egosystem" instead of an "ecosystem." Evidence is accumulating to show that many individuals do *not* adapt— that they are incapable of becoming anonymous, mechanized, computerized, dehumanized *Homo technos.* They cut out of the system: They return to the biosphere in communes; they seek rural occupations—handicrafts, pottery, farming. Others feel a loss of meaningful personal interaction and they join growth groups—T groups—or they get involved in local welfare and urban action programs. All this indicates that certain needs of the individual *will* inevitably surface when the system does not provide them with outlets. These men and women may protect their children from materialistic programming and, instead, sensitize them to an awareness of things as they are in the biosphere.

Our children must be shown their place in the ecosystem and become detached from the global egosystem in which *Homo technos* has trapped himself and which, out of narcissism and the fear of the unknown, he feels impelled to preserve and develop. The child is distinct from an adult. He can be taught by example not to strive to express his fantasies and projections materially through technology. Without detachment from the egosystem he might envisage a beautiful arch or an enormous factory, and in order to build and maintain it, drain physical energy from the biosphere and contribute only pollution. Such minds parasitize the physical energy of the earth, which is being rapaciously depleted at a feverish speed in order that such materialistic dreams may be realized in the name of progress, profit and national pride.

The biosphere is being depleted by *Homo technos* at work evolving his own technosphere and is constantly being drained of energy to support his artifacts and systems. Ultimately, not at doomsday but at *birthday,* these artifacts and values alike will decay and become shells, like abandoned pyramids and temples, as man's spirit moves him on to grow in a different dimension and to embrace a different set of values and goals. Already we see highly educated young people quitting the cities and children in day schools talking of conservation. A whole new set of values and a readjusted need hierarchy is emerging in the younger generation. They can perhaps thank the establishment people who have spent their lives developing and maintaining the ruins that surround us now, threatening our very existence, for having shown them the limitations of this evolutionary cul-de-sac.

The economist will say we need a technology to support a growing population. I would say simply limit the population growth and educate the public, and we will no longer need such a consumer-oriented technology. And anyway, we have so much overproduction now that we have to *create* a market for many products through another megaindustry—consumer advertising.

These value systems are obviously sick. Consider that Western man per capita consumes more raw materials and physical energy than do those of any other culture; he is clearly out of balance with the energy available in the biosphere. Why must *Homo technos* live at such a peak of affluence—an affluence not necessary to the normal fulfillment of his basic biological needs? Surely a man who has everything spiritually, who has everything he needs in his social relationships and has come to terms with and is deeply happy with himself, needs little more. He doesn't need "life-supportive" toys like flamboyant cars, a prestige home in the "right" community, expensive "labour-saving" gadgetry from an automatic lawn mower to a vast deep freeze, half a dozen telephones throughout the house, individual color television sets for family members, and so on. Luxury items to other cultures have become his barest necessities—necessities he spends his whole life working to obtain and maintain. Certainly they are conveniences, and yet they are also voracious consumers of energy, components of a system that is gravely out of balance with nature, but perhaps not so with the insatiable needs of those individuals who support it. These materialistic needs are insatiable because they are merely placebos, temporarily quieting the deeper inner need for *more being* that they alone can never satisfy. And then there is pure laziness; physical work is not fulfilling but demeaning!

The few remaining tribes of primitive peoples who have not yet been contaminated by the culture of *Homo technos* have comparatively few needs. In modern man we find a multiplicity of new ones—all socially acquired. They are associated with man's materialism and with the increasing complexity of wants and dependencies that can cause not only continued striving, confusion, and conflict, but that also and invariably draw the individual away from a more self-actualizing or fulfilling path of development.

When there is increasing complexity in the technocratic society, there is often a decreasing diversity in its relation with the biosphere. Consider the early hunter-gatherer societies: They were not complex, and yet the ecology supporting their biological needs for food resources was both complex and diverse. This is dramatically illustrated by the Shoshone Indians, who utilized no less than one hundred forty different food plants. Diversity is crucially important because with it man doesn't put all his eggs in one basket, relying on one or two major food sources. With great diversity a disease that might wipe out a particular crop species might not necessarily affect others. A bad season might deplete some, but man's entire resources would not be wiped out. As soon as man ceased to be a hunter-gatherer and became more sedentary, he had to limit his universe in order to control it. When he tried to take over and control nature, he did not have sufficient knowledge to do so. And consequently, he narrowed his universe and focused his attention on only a few species of plants and animals which he eventually domesticated, namely the cereals and hoofed animals, especially cattle, sheep, goats, pigs, and horses for work. He also forgot much of what he knew when he was part of nature and set out on a perilous new evolutionary path. Later, he could not get off it because of the responsibilities he'd assumed of a growing populace dependent on the new narrowed way of life.

Taking this new road was at the outset an ecological catastrophe for man, one which he is now attempting to rectify. Hunting-gathering societies rarely experienced famine except in more extreme climates such as the Arctic, whereas agrarian man has frequently done so, not just because he lived at a much higher population density, but also because he lacked diversity of food sources, so that with a drought his entire crops could be blighted, or with a disease all his livestock could be wiped out. With this future-oriented anxiety, new religions flourished to appease man's global neurosis and existential uncertainty: With progress came mental anguish.

In contrast to this harrowed relation with the biosphere, increasing technological evolution has seen a greater and greater increase in the complexity of social structure and of technological interdependencies, from the extreme poles of the producer and consumer through the wholesaler, the retailer, the contractor, the one who finds the raw materials, the one who sells them to the one who processes, the one who builds component parts, the one who assembles them, and the one who now recycles used parts. More and more niches, or roles for people, were provided in the technology as its internal structure became more complex and more diverse. In a sense this was a mirror image of the interdependence and dynamic balance of the biosphere, or natural ecology, that evolving man was leaving behind. The biosphere, as utilized by man, now tended, as we have seen, to be extremely monolithic, only a few species of plants and animals being kept. Even the genetic diversity of different types of high-producing hybrids have their limits, and we are clearly pushing those limits, as it is extremely difficult now to produce new strains of corn that will be resistant to the various viruses and fungi to which they are susceptible.

Jane Jacobs, in her book entitled *The Economy of Cities,* makes a similar point, namely that there has been an increase in technological diversity, providing more niches, or roles and opportunities, for people residing in cities. In the technosphere a new product may fill a new niche and a market or need may be created for it. Several niches may form a basis for more and so on, exponentially, so that within our technology there is an increasing potential for diversity and for continued growth: A lesson from nature that we should also apply to agriculture or to our "domesticated" biosphere. But unlike the natural biosphere, our artificial ecologies are not balanced and self-contained. They are exploitative of, and dependent on, natural resources, unremittingly depleting and polluting the biosphere.

Variations are created in the technosphere through differentiated production. We do need to return to this kind of diversity in our *agricultural practices and general management of the biosphere* so that our products and resources are more supple, more diverse, and can flex with famine, disease, and with changing market needs.

We are reaching the limits of diversity or possible diversification within the species of plants and animals we have domesticated. We must look more to a new and different relationship with the biosphere. We must foster greater diversity, explore possibilities, and try to establish once again the more harmonious relationship the hunter-gatherers had with their environment, a greater oneness as part of the great mosaic in which there was diversity, equilibrium, and yet flexibility. Consider the early agrarians who knew their crops could be wiped out by drought; so they would make a rain god. They needed the sun for their crops as well; so they would make a sun god, and so on. In this way further diversity evolved within the culture insofar as religions were concerned. The Hopi Indians had many gods, or spirits, for different functions and for support for their anxieties —anxieties arising because of their insecure relationship with the artificial universe they were creating for themselves. This kind of religion is a religion based on future fear—the fear that we *might* have famine; the crops *might* fail. As man became future-oriented, he became increasingly anxious and neurotic. His religion and his psychological makeup came to differ greatly from

A different pace of life: American & Indian, contrasts the impersonal insanity of urban automania and the intensely personal environment of an "undeveloped" country. The fruits of progress are of questionable worth.

those of the primitives, who were more at one with their environment.

The primitive went more with the flow of his environment and with the seasons, while civilized man pushed against the river, against the flow of things, because he attempted to control—to control the part of the biosphere he had begun to domesticate. And so, perhaps, with the development of agriculture and of civilization as we know it, man began to develop the real neuroses and paranoid religions we still have today. Religions based on anxiety and fear are obviously less desirable than those based more on a natural sense of wonder and a spiritual faith in one's relationships to the known and to the unknown of the wilderness.

In the context of this discussion, then, the more needs that arose as modern man made his technological society more complex, the more confusion, the more stress, and the more anxieties created by one generation as legacy for the next.

What, if any, are the solutions? *Reverence for all life*—animal, plant, and human—is a beginning, together with concerted conservation efforts to protect the biosphere from further pollution and exploitation. But in the face of dire human needs conservation will inevitably take a lower priority. It will take second place until two categories of human needs and values are changed: The first is population growth and the second is technological growth, which, in Eastern and Western hemispheres respectively, are biocidal cancers. In the West the spiral pathology of production-trade-consumption, the creation of new industries to employ more people to produce more "things," so they in turn can have more things, more time (freedom?), money, power, etc., is an illusion. The post-technological age to come will see this as the monster of the twentieth century. The socioeconomic and political-corporate military complexes of international trade, balance of payments, power and progress, coupled with the inevitable stratification of society within nation states, with division of labor, status striving, inequality, and union strikes, seem a dear price to pay for progress and growth. A new ethic of "small is beautiful," rather than "bigger and more are better," is needed. It will complement conservation efforts and the ethic of reverence for all life. With such ethical responsibilities the quality of human life will improve, since human values and priorities will change and man may then discover greater fulfillment.

11

Social and Psychological
Aspects of Ecology

In a small band of our hunter-gatherer forefathers, there would have been a very limited diversity of roles as well as needs. In our modern society we have multitudes of different roles, and within them are multitudes of people who, in these conceptual spaces, have essentially different realities, or *Umwelts*. We can speak, therefore, of "separate realities" in relation to the ecology of the mind.

A person in his niche can feel in control if he knows all its facts. One can be a specialist in a science merely by reading a few papers published in an esoteric area. He then becomes one of a few world experts. In attempting to maintain his position of information-awareness, he experiences the stress and anxiety of attempting to keep up with new developments in that area and of possibly missing something that might be pertinent. One way of avoiding this type of future shock is to become a *super*specialist, to refine one's niche, to narrow it down to an even more specialized area encompassing less information. Consequently a person will have a greater sense of security and identity until he generates sufficient information himself to influence others, who will then begin to produce more facts and grow conceptually upon what he has provided as a base. Then, ultimately, he will become completely immersed in things that rise above *his* head, and then he will retire. If he holds on, he is likely to make a fool of himself, if not destroy his earlier, established reputation! This specialization, especially among scientists and technologists, can be a very precarious way of life. It is akin to an individual identifying himself solely with what he does—with his role. (Ask such a person, "Who are *you*?" The reply is invariably not who he *is* but what he *does*.)

The problem of overspecialization in the ecology of the mind is very real. In becoming a specialist one narrows the number of doors one can open. One begins to limit opportunities. With increasing overspecialization there is increasing inflexibility, and so one becomes more and more embedded in a given niche or, in another sense, in one particular way of thinking, relating, and being. It is so secure and reassuring to be in a stable environment with few variables that one can fairly efficiently control and predict. To jump out involves courage and risk-taking. Change requires faith, confidence, self-esteem, and detachment from one's own ego investments. We have examples from our animal brothers of the problems of this kind of overspecialization. For example, the koala bear is biologically overspecialized, he can survive only on eucalyptus shoots. Similarly, the panda bear cannot go where bamboo shoots do not grow. Becoming a specialist and demanding a single kind of food limits an animal's potential. It cannot exploit the diversity of its environment. The same is true of the human being whose mind becomes so overspecialized he can no longer exploit or explore the diversity of things around him. He becomes stuck, a prisoner in his own conceptual and perceptual field. (Holding to the same analogy, we see this overspecialization in the domestication of animals. Consider the various breeds of dogs as a genetic analogy to the cultural specializion we see in man.)

It is well worth reflecting on the possibility that where certain cultures might not regard a particular material as food, another may see the same thing as a staple diet. So it is with the limitation of a conceptual mind within its own niche. The limits of its perceptions determine how the person will feel and react when circumstances around him force him out of or destroy his own conceptual world. Like the koala bear deprived of eucalyptus, the narrow mind, when forced out of its small niche, can conceive of nowhere else to go. There is a great sense of total loss and aloneness.

We must not raise our children to be conceptually conservative and burdened with narrow perspectives. While the koala bear is conservative innately or genetically, many people's cultures are conservative in relation to their beliefs, through *social* rather than genetic programming. The conservative mind, the closed tape loop, and the inflexible personality type limited to a small universe has limited potential. Worse still is its inability to adapt to change. With the rapid rate of change going on around us at the moment, if a person does not keep abreast (or, rather than attempting to do that, go with the flow and remain flexible), he will not be able to adapt. And after a time change will make his own conceptual niche redundant. He will become obsolete, but in order to feel safe and to preserve his identity, he clings on to where he is. Generations ago a man would perhaps pass his entire working life without becoming obsolete, yet now a person who develops specific skills might find himself outmoded in as little as five years. He then has to go through the entire process of rehabilitation and relocation in a new job after he has been reprogrammed to fit into a new niche.

Additionally, if we are going to produce such specialists who deal only on the surface with skills and information, we will be producing technologists rather than human beings who are basically far more flexible, who can go with the flow, and so who can better adapt to change. Are we even now producing such humanoids, pathological specialists who must be stripped down and reprogrammed every five or ten years to meet the new demands of a changing technology? And will the normal ones who resist early programming become extinct?

Since there is so much competition for conceptual niches in this mind-ecology, as soon as one obtains a niche, one may defend it violently. And in paranoid defense and anxiety, one convinces himself that the value of that niche automatically increases. The need to defend oneself in this way is certainly related to an over-evolvement of the ego in that conceptual reality. When a person perceives his ego defenses, he becomes aware of his previous folly and is able to move out and explore new possibilities. Many people, however, find themselves trapped permanently in the separate realities of their own conceptual niches, for which they have competed so keenly. And the competition around them *keeps* them in their niches and makes them fight fiercely to preserve them. Admittedly the great diversity of niches or of opportunities in modern society is more desirable in many ways than the limited ones in more primitive cultures, where lack of means to develop certain skills and creative potential could be extremely self-limiting and repressive. The individual in a complex society has a greater chance at finding a niche that is compatible with his own desires and abilities. However, there is a limit to the number of niches available in relation to the population, so people begin to struggle for places, and this competition sets in as soon as they enter school. Such competition can make life more of a cutthroat rat race than a cooperative experience.

It is easy to see that when the specialized mind contracts into a niche and so limits its universe in order to focus all energies on the task or role involved, the whole, or Gestalt, cannot be perceived. The person does not see himself as part of a far greater whole. He may rationalize and say he is centred upon himself, but his level of awareness is drastically limited to a microcosm which he, in the center, believes to be the entire universe. The important thing is to integrate levels of awareness and knowledge. We have different people in different niches, and if they could only become more aware of one another and integrate their diverse knowledge, they would continue to grow and enrich one another at an incredible rate. As it is, most people get their minds frozen in these conceptual niches quite early on, and this limits their growth potential. It places a ceiling on their beliefs, and when they feel they have achieved or experienced the ultimate, they have only hit the edge of their universe, which is the thin wall of their entombing droplet of awareness—a microcosm in a vast galactic continuum of consciousness.

Once a person recognizes that he is playing a role and that he identifies (as do others) with what he does, rather than with what he is, he may be able to break out of his mind trap. He may find the strength and personal commitment to move out of that perceptually limiting microcosm and so discover the freedom for further growth and self-actualization. He is able to rediscover himself and his individuality, which is lost in the isolation of what he does. The termite of the social machine becomes a man. Individuality is the Gestalt, the sum of all qualities that make up the entire person. Add to this the awareness of the complexity of different conceptual levels and their many niches, which make up the whole ecology of the mind. Then one can see a whole universe of consciousness as an interconnected matrix where all minds can be linked.

Diversity of the mind must be fostered for human evolution; monolithic thinking could be as disastrous as an agricultural monoculture. But with diversity we must have unity in shared meta-values and common goals for humanity. The diverse biosphere is an integrated ecosystem. Each animal and plant has its place, whether it is a host or parasite, whether it is prey or predator. There is balance, harmony, equilibrium and enough instability for growth and change. So man at the psychic level must move toward this state of harmony, where many diverse minds, instead of being isolated in separate realities that create a void of confusion, can come together into an integrated ecology of the mind, the noösphere of collective consciousness. This may be potentiated through an opening up of the collective unconscious, according to Jung, which must be linked with the supraconscious Gestalt vision of wholeness and unity within diversity and individuality—the paradox that both ecologist and Zen master perceive.

Politics and Consciousness

As Charles Reich pointed out in his book *The Greening of America,* in the world today there is not primarily an economic depression, but a depression of the spirit of humanity. We have

an anthill developing out of an enormous, anonymous technological society. Teilhard de Chardin observed that in some of
these mounds communism replaces brotherly love with an identification with the collective—not a psychic or spiritual collective,
but a materialistic one. With democracy capitalism makes brothers compete and destroy each other, while fascism restricts brotherhood to a chosen few. Dr. F. L. K. Hsu, in an article entitled
"American Core Value and National Character" in a text on
cross-cultural psychiatry,* shows that in the democratic society
of America there is a schizophrenic dualism in many of our basic
values, such as Christian love versus religious bigotry; emphasis
on science, progress, and humanitarianism versus parochialism,
group superiority, and racism. We find a schizophrenia between
our Puritan ethics on the one hand and an increased laxity in
sexual mores on the other. Also democratic ideals of equality and
freedom are in sharp contrast to our totalitarian dependencies,
witch-hunting, and so on.

No politically organized society, be it communist, democratic,
or fascist, has yet reached an ideal stage of evolution in terms of
the welfare of both individual and the society and yet each is
converging on the same position from different points, so that
hopefully both society and the individual will ultimately be more
healthy and differences between political values will be past
history.

Corporate capitalism can, as we have seen, become an exploitation of undeveloped nations in order to feed an already overdeveloped, overproductive society that must create markets for
new products and is at the same time polluting and depleting the
biosphere. Corporate systems remain viable by enforcing conformity and encouraging ilusory "freedom." The individual's personal life merges with his public life and, as Charles Reich points
out, an employee may essentially sell out to the system that in return rewards him with status and a false sense of security, identity,
and material reward. The more he is promoted, the more status
but less personal freedom he possesses. His individuality (who he

---

* F. L. K. Hsu (editor), *Psychological Anthropology,* Dorsey Press, 1961.

is) is lost to individualism (what he does, i.e., professionalism). Ultimately he exchanges his own self-identity for a group identity or collective ego of the corporate empire. Others in lower echelons might envy those who achieve power and esteem in workers' unions, executive committees, and boards of directors. But theirs is not a true unity or brotherhood; it is based merely on an impersonal, dehumanizing materialistic egosystem, and therefore is part of the larger system they support and that controls them. As in the termite mound there is a hierarchy, a caste system, a division of labor, but little sense of humanity or brotherly love.

Traditionally in the past workers (for basic material needs) and intellectuals (for humanistic needs) have united in revolution against capitalism and corporate control. But a true socialism has rarely emerged because there are always leaders, and a new hierarchical system usually replaces the old. When the power wielders of a technological society control the mass media and all communication systems, the subservient, supportive populace can be totally manipulated. Public opinion can be altered overnight, and militant forces attempting to bring about social change can be crushed. Technocrats can, therefore, control the evolution of society, be their control beneficial or detrimental.

Our modern mobile society has few truly stable and organized communities and, consequently, is not organized for coordinated group political action. Nor are the needs of the individuals fully heard or met by our political structure and by our political representatives. They will make pre-election promises, but the promises are rarely fulfilled. We can begin to develop our own communications systems by starting at the interpersonal level within small groups and so develop a greater collective sense of being and of belonging. Through the encounter group we might develop a more socially relevant and sensitized nucleus for future political action. We are seeing this already in women's lib and gay-lib and, before them, in conservation and humane society organizations. Small groups of people, be they homosexuals, women wishing independence, groups of black people, or white Caucasian males also desiring liberation from their own stereotypes, are springing up all over the United States. A gradual *internal* change is even now occurring, and the process of hominization or rehumanization of technologized man is accelerating in this "counterculture" movement.

We must congratulate ourselves on the enormous diversity we have developed in our technosphere. However, it has not yet evolved to the degree of integration we see in the biosphere—nor have we. When we can have equilibrium within the technosphere, then we will no longer have problems of pollution. Biological ecologies are complex integrated systems. We must strive to achieve the same model in the final evolution of our technology for "spaceship earth," and we may also realize this same state for our minds.

Teilhard de Chardin, in an eloquent discourse, refers to these three levels as the biosphere, the technosphere, and the noösphere (see Figure 2, Chapter 10). Admittedly, too, with increasing diversity in the technosphere we have increased our conceptual diversity. Many of these mind-niches are, however, still at a relatively low materialistic level, and we must strive further for more spiritual levels of awareness.

Growth and Change

We might pause to wonder what the trigger was that caused the phenomenon of agriculture to develop in so many different places all over the world, and all at more or less the same time. As soon as man stepped out of his relationship with the natural world as a hunter-gatherer and became agrarian, he experienced for the first time a tension caused by a disequilibrium between himself and the artificial ecology he was developing. Here, in a very pessimistic view, one could say that when this kind of evolutionary step occurred, there was instability at the outset, and the very term "progress" is not in essence progress, but rather an attempt to counter this instability and to restore stability and harmony between man and nature. But this may be impossible since nature has now been so transformed that much of it is artificial or man-made. Man must therefore come to terms with *himself* since what is without is a mirror of the chaos within!

The advent of technology was at the beginning, in the true ecological sense, a pathological maladaptation, and much progress to date has taken us farther away from being able to restore equilibrium. The tension between the individual and society coupled with its technology may well be the progressive stimulus to advancement. Once a stable point of equilibrium is attained, will there be no further "progress" in the real sense but entropy? Will this be heralded by a gradual decline from affluence to decay? Did the great cultures of the past—China and Egypt, for example—reach a point of stability, become complex but closed systems with no open doors, and gradually implode? Do we need this progressive kind of pathological disequilibrium and tension to keep the system open to continued development?

I do not think this is the only way we can evolve. In all developmental processes there is not only direction, but there is also flexibility linked with diversity. And in each stage of development there is integration. What we must do now is begin to integrate our minds in their different ecological niches and integrate all the diverse but interdependent parts of our technology, so that one small part cannot run away and become cancerous and pollute or otherwise destroy the rest of the system, just like a sick mind in the ecosystem of the psyche could similarly destroy others.

This tension between the culture and the newly evolving technology was a stimulus to continued development. We have a good example of this in modern agriculture, where we are now at a stage with our corn crops of having to monitor nearly every trace element, every insect, and every virus and fungus that comes near our plants. In the old days we could let things be for some insects would buffer others and protect specific plants, and there would be sufficiently diverse plants in the soil to insure it would remain fertile. And there was no attempt to overproduce on those wild acres. As man took them over and made them less diverse, however, he had to assume greater and greater responsibility for the small parts that made up that ecosystem—the small parts, right down to the trace elements and viruses. His universe had shrunk, but this microcosm nevertheless overwhelmed him in its complexity, and, because of this, modern man is a reductionist.

He is concerned with analyzing, predicting, and controlling the small parts that seem to determine his very future. And as a consequence of this tuning of his mind, very few individuals are able to see the whole—to see the whole of the very small universe that is the technosphere and to see man's folly and to discover solutions.

Similarly, perhaps, the tension between the individual and his culture evokes an energy or stimulus to creative activity. He attempts to reduce the dissonance or the discordance between his own personal needs and the needs and values imposed on him and the opportunities available in his culture. With increasing complexity, according to Teilhard de Chardin, there is increasing consciousness, and this a valid law of evolution. We can see, therefore, that with increasing complexity in our technology, we are evolving. But without integration (with biosphere and noösphere) society will be merely an unintegrated cancerous mass. Teilhard and others note that the natural world (biosphere) has been relatively at an evolutionary standstill for hundreds of thousands of years, except for minute changes here and there. This is because complexity has reached its ultimate point in the various ecosystems. The systems become closed; there is a ceiling to complexity. In our technology, too, we may be reaching a limit to the degree of complexity possible. Will this also limit the complexity and, therefore, the diversity of possible opportunities for people of different interests and natural talents? We must also think of personal development—that in an environment providing great enrichment and complexity one's consciousness will be elevated, but only when experiences at different stages of one's life are integrated. This, again, is the positive point of psychoanalysis, of merging or reintegrating past experiences that have been pushed back into the unconscious. It is essentially setting a person back on the growth path so that we have an individual no longer limiting his universe, and therefore making his experiences less complex. His consciousness and his awareness will also be limited no longer. We do not, however, need a complex technology to help us gain a greater degree of awareness about the nature of things, but as Teilhard and Charles Reich have shown, technology can be a stepping-stone to free man from environmental demands and to free him for his own personal growth and continued evolution.

The contemporary crises in the ecology of the mind—the increase of mental illness—and in the ecology of the biosphere—growing pollution—may in fact be positive stimuli to evolution. (An act of conservation is consciousness-raising in action.) Mankind and nations will find unity in the ecological crises to come, and a global consciousness of humanity—the noösphere—will evolve from this. These crises, the symptoms of the times, are but fleeting moments in the eonic cycle of cosmic evolution. Man is on the crest of this tidal wave of time and change. Unlike any animal on this earth before him, he alone can see his past and, to an increasing extent, see and control his future. Man's destiny rests on his own decisions now. So much of the world around him reflects his inner being—in chaos, suffering, and beauty alike. The imprint of man on nature is his mirror, and as man evolves and matures, so his outer world will change and become more perfect with each generation. As a man thinks, so he is.

The ravaged wilderness and ravaged minds alike mirror each other today. Science has become the religion of technological man, who worships false gods and is enamoured of his own creations, like Narcissus before a mirror. Adam and Eve left the Garden of Eden, not because they were banished by an angry god, but because they had evolved beyond animals into a higher level of consciousness. No, an apple didn't give them that knowledge after one bite! And so they, being neither animal nor god, were alone in the wilderness. Tomorrow we may realize that we are both animals and gods in terms of our basic needs, feelings, and higher awareness and responsibility for our own destiny and for the future of this world. Today man separates himself from both animals and God and is trapped in the worship of his own creations. If a man can free himself from this trap—like the tar pits and overspecialization that led to the extinction of other species before him—he may realize his full "polymorphous" potential.

How can one open the doors of perception and discover God

within and heaven on earth? To become a transpersonal, transcultural being freed from culturally biassed seeing and valuing
will open the door to collective awareness, to the global brotherhood of the noösphere. In order to grow up (evolve) a man must
grow out of his culture (out of his dependencies and insecurities),
out of that mould casting him into a predetermined shape, like
Karma. Those who hold on can neither live nor die. Such is hell
on earth, a state of limbo for a man, a cultural species who,
being neither animal nor god, is therefore nothing. He will be a
cosmic joke, a fragment of evolutionary flotsam whose bones and
endeavours alike will lie forgotten on the shores of time. Can such
Homo technos, who is destroying himself and therefore nature,
ever *learn* from nature? It would seem such men of action cannot; but instead, like children, they will have to learn from their
mistakes. Can they transcend the burden (Karma) of their own
actions and civilization through intellect per se, since faith alone
is not enough? The answer is in each and all of us.

The principles of the ecologist and a wealth of data from
ecological studies—the relationships between plant and animal,
prey and predator, population size and food supply—are pertinent in studying the synthetic man-made ecologies of our cities
and industries, as well as the biological impact of the human
species on the natural ecology. We must hold in check the biocidal activities of a naïve animal who has suddenly developed
technological skills, and yet is dangerously ignorant of its relationship to the biosphere and the possible outcome of its tech-
nomania, and who has seen the systems and machines it creates
begin to take control, much like Frankenstein's monster. We do
not need a return to simplicity, but a restoration of stability to
permit reorganization from within—cultural and economic unity
based on greater equality of opportunity and fair distribution of
both wealth and resources.

Once we can rid ourselves of the irrational, egocentric, arrogant
assumption acquired from our pioneer ancestors—that we, as
a species, are a law unto ourselves, and that we have been
created as an entity distinct from and with dominion over other

Many die anonymously in the name of peace or for political causes they do not comprehend, while social change, to prevent such collective insanity, too often sparks radical flames and establishment retribution. Man has not yet learned to live as a truly social and humane being: a desecrated hillside eloquently displays the truth.

life forms—we may shuck off our present cultural chains. If not, destruction and decay seem otherwise inevitable.

Arrogant or escapist followers of some religions have the answer—believe, and man will be saved for the *next* world while this one goes to hell. If not indifferent, they remain passive, conforming to socially accepted roles. Their sin is passivity, the sin of omission, the sin of the uncommitted who, in caring only for themselves, cannot see beyond their immediate needs. They have the illusion that they are "free" men, and this illusion sustains them through life.

God is nature and nature is order, a complex interrelated system in which each component is dependent. And each dependency involves mutual obligation at the level of awareness attained in man. Man, in his attempt to separate himself from "lower" forms and from nature, personifies God and, in so doing, separates himself from nature and his fellow beings alike. With a personified God who judges, forgives, and takes care of things, how easy it then is to abdicate responsibility to others and to oneself. Easy then, today as in the past, for church or state to take over this responsibility, to subjugate and manipulate the masses who prefer servitude and control to the terrible freedom of responsibility. But freedom without responsibility is an illusion. A free man is independent or, rather, "nondependent." He may be judged nonconformist or radical revolutionist. One was once crucified, yet few understood his message and lived as he dared.

An example of one of the dilemmas of civilized man is population control versus religious teachings and tradition. Freed from outmoded religious teachings that promise heaven to those who propagate like global parasites, many now recognize the threat of overpopulation and rigorously control family size. Man has no natural predatorial enemy (except himself), and so there are no biological controls of his numbers, unless we accept war, disease, and famine as "natural" control mechanisms. At one time it was politically expedient to spawn a majority; birth control was condemned and special concessions and social status were accorded larger families. Subsequently it became a deeprooted socioreligious custom to breed a large family—and so it is more difficult at the present time to effect some kind of reform through education or actual state enforcement. India, for example, claims today that it does not have a population crisis but, rather, a shortage of food. It rightly blames the Western world for overconsumption but is, like a neurotic, blind to its own problems. Possibly early experience may influence a child's preference in adulthood for a particular number of offspring; those from large families may not be able to see themselves in a small family of one or two, and therefore prefer that *their* offspring have many brothers and sisters. In Catholic-dominated countries people continue to proliferate, encouraged and blessed by their papal gamekeeper.

In nature the more successful animals are those that obtain breeding territory and mating partners. Physically or genetically inferior and younger individuals do not breed. Looking at the dilemma in man, both nationally and internationally, we see the reversal of this propagation priority that occurs in nature; the less educated (and possibly the less desirable genetic combinations?*) have more offspring, and in a democracy this could be disastrous if such majorities determine national policies and control consensus values. A democracy can only be fully effective when all are educated to the highest ethical values and responsible, compassionate, rational attitudes. In a national election, for example, the majority vote may have severe repercussions if the majority are poorly educated, prejudiced, and misinformed.

If the informed, the educated, and the concerned breed less and become a dwindling minority, will they be swamped by those who are the worker ants, subservient to corporate technophiles who keep them ignorant and dependent "for their own good"? And so a nation misled by opportunistic politicians begins to erode internally—a goodly apple rotten at the core. The only obvious solution may be revolution or war, but the real solution is an educational "motivation" in human consciousness.

---

* Although I believe that it is the "genes" of ideas, attitudes, and values in our consciousness rather than the actual genes that are epigenetically man's key to fulfillment—or self-destruction.

Shrouded in political and religious ideals, morality is difficult to define. An individual may act out of conviction or belief and feel his action was moral. Biologically it may be immoral, but moral in terms of his religious training; such is the problem with sex and the single pope, where religious "moral" teaching can become immoral through ignorance of biological "morality." Moral responsibility changes as each generation changes in an evolving technological society. But we apply outmoded codes generations later—now, when population density is dangerously high, and when religion has not evolved into something more meaningful to an educated, scientifically minded populace. The population explosion could be reduced by condoning the use of contraceptives. And to deny man his freedom to apply scientific knowledge to control his own ecology—a necessity with man becoming less and less dependent on natural biological selection —is immoral. Supporters of such outmoded religious morality might well say that epidemics, famines, and war are natural— unfortunate, but part of human nature. Must they let these be our only pruning shears to reduce our growing numbers so only the "fittest" will survive?

Of all people the teacher has the highest moral responsibility. This high morality must operate in complete academic freedom— the freedom to express ideas—and cannot function when religious or political pressures are imposed to control or question academic freedom in relation to current religious or political doctrines. Too many teachers—the Greeks and latter-day European professors— moulded their students after them, catching their genius at second or third hand, and never allowing the students' own genius to bloom. Their growth had been shaped and restricted, their progress limited. They were disciples of a discipline whose evolution was delayed or arrested because the student had to assimilate, conform, never question the master. Such restrictions on growth and change were also imposed by religious and political powers, and to question was heresy. How far may one question today and get a truthful answer? Throughout the history of man education has been polluted by political indoctrination of the young, and this perversion through education is the most powerful and immoral weapon man has turned upon himself.

Today's student (and, in some schools, tomorrow's) should be free to question; this they can only do when they have some facts, some insight, and freedom to express their opinions. Education is a subtle combination of factual discipline and conceptual freedom. To destroy this freedom is to destroy progress and to spawn a generation of conformists, or disciples of mediocrity.

It is responsible freedom that is the quality of mature humanness, combining compassionate action with reverence for all life. Such ethically responsible being is surely the key to human fulfillment and peace on earth.

Peace is derived from order. In nature this order is termed the balance of nature, whereas in man it is the balance of power. To be at peace is therefore a dynamic process in which there is an understanding between the individual and his own society, and also among societies or nations. In order to maintain peace this understanding must keep pace with developmental changes within and between individuals, societies, and nations alike. Where evolution (change) is taking place because of some new economic reform or political or religious movement, the values of individuals change, too, as do their perception and ways of thinking. Conflicting values and desires between peoples should no longer be resolved through war, but the rights of minorities must be protected. A peace army may one day be needed, directed by an international or world government. Before this world government can ever be established, however, a world majority would have to acquire the wisdom of nature to understand the nature of man and thus be at once effective and humane.

We must develop such wisdom in order to direct our own future since we have become almost completely emancipated from the normal regulating controls of nature, our technology having disrupted the natural processes that once regulated population growth. Heaven will be on earth when man attains self-control collectively and restores a state of balance between the worlds of nature and man, animals and resources, human desires and power.

Human Potential

The human species, a product of evolution, has the power of re-creation. Man can project and express in the outer world his inner landscape of dreams and ideas through words or material forms (art, architecture, tools, and machines). With computer technology he has ultimately simulated himself, a complete facsimile or re-creation of his own rational consciousness. Clearly all things are possible within the limits of consciousness: Nothing that can be conceived cannot be ultimately expressed materially. Perhaps the human need always to be doing something (creation), to explore the outer limits of physical and conceptual space, is a ceaseless striving.

Some have dubbed mankind *Homo ludens,* the playful, forever seeking recreation or, in this sense, re-creation. Why? Is there no end to such ceaseless activity? All artifacts, concepts, and beliefs can be built upon and transcended—all is transient, mortal. The possibilities are infinite, as in the way our minds reflect the infinity of outer space. Each generation is like a stepping-stone, each a link. As we learn from the elders, so our children learn from us and move on into conceptual realities we may never fully comprehend. Consciousness also "in-volves," turns in on itself, and is reflective. It is analogous to a reflection, a hologram of the cosmos, since the more that is within (that which is known or conceived), the more there is without (that which can be perceived). As a man sees, so he is.

Inborn concepts or *engrams,* the archetypal memories of Carl Jung, provide the template for the exponential growth of consciousness, both in the individual and in the culture's collective consciousness. Once there is self- or reflective consciousness, there is self-direction and self-determination (free will). Psychic (mental) evolution is superimposed on physical evolution, which may remain relatively unchanged over many generations (i.e., evolution of matter is followed by evolution of consciousness). Even so, psychic evolution within the ecology of mind is still affected by laws similar to those that influence physical evolution, namely adaptation, "fitness," diversity, and specialization, in spite of self-determining "freedom."

The end point of biological (physical) evolution is the beginning of psychic development, so that the evolutionary process recreates itself in consciousness.* Man can re-create himself and his own life through an awareness of the dimensions and potential of his consciousness. Imagine the moment when the first caveman drew an animal form on the rock face! On this new evolutionary trajectory new worlds (conceptual realities) can be conceived and creatively expressed. Teilhard de Chardin refers to this as "psychic interiorization" or "cosmic convolution," a turning in or reflection of the evolutionary process.

As in the past, when certain species lacking the physical qualities to survive perished through natural selection, so today natural/social selection works against certain personality or psychological types in man.† Some should be protected, not only for humane reasons but also for the evolutionary necessity of maintaining diversity, even though the society at any given time may reinforce only one particular type because of its monolithic institutions of values, concepts, and skills. All human minds may not adapt to such limiting niches, and sanctuary should be provided for those who cannot find a prescribed or alternative niche.

Worse, perhaps, is the more widespread entrapment of human consciousness, in which the mind gets caught and controlled by the processes of evolution (development, change, and action), instead of being in control as the processor. In other words, the player gets lost in the game ("doing" instead of "being"), whereas, ideally, he should write the script and be both player and observer. The almost schizoid humor of Zen reflects this subjective-objective shift in awareness/involvement from serious, striving player to detached and impartial, nonstriving observer. Either is an illusory trap.

Evolution at the psychic level is therefore a combination of evolution and involution—expression, introspection, and impres-

---

* By analogy, therefore, genes perform the same function at the physical level as do concepts and plans at the mental level.

† Does contemporary Western society not favor a competitive, aggressive, assertive individualistic personality type? Hardly a cooperative and supportive tribal brother!

sion; creation, reflection, and recreation. There is increasing complexity and synthesis, increasing diversity and unity. The eternal paradox of the All in One and the One in All.

12

Animal and Human Awareness;
Superiority and Racism

"Dogs are surely more intelligent than cats, and German shepherds and greyhounds are superior to mongrels." Many people would accept such a statement without question, but might balk at "Whites are more intelligent than blacks, and a mathematician or doctor is superior to a car mechanic or a gardener." Or would they? I am often asked if dogs are indeed more intelligent than cats, and I counter the question by pointing out that the end point of such linear thinking is a racist conclusion. In essence, there is nothing better for a cat to be than a cat. Also, if we attempted to measure the learning abilities of cat versus dog, we would have difficulty in setting up fair measures since the dog has some specialized abilities the cat does not have, and vice versa. Dogs are more dependent than most cats, more eager to please their masters, and therefore easier to train.

Motivation can also affect the validity of an IQ test, since what interests a dog may not turn the cat on to perform at all. Emotions interfere with learning tests, too. For example, fear or timidity can inhibit an animal from responding, and extreme excitement can impair performance. Additionally, the monitor may not be aware that a test subject performs well because it has been in a similar situation before. Conversely, it may do poorly because of some early emotional trauma that set up a phobia that is reactivated by a particular test situation (such as responding to a loud bell or learning a way out of a maze in a subject that is sound-shy or afraid of confinement, respectively). Being raised in a restricted environment (a cage or kennel) may also influence an animal's performance.

So many factors can interfere with any "objective" test of intelligence that it is difficult to compare one dog with another, let alone a cat and a dog. Even if we could design a fair battery of tests allowing for individual and species differences ("specialist" traits and physical limitations) and for differences in emotionality and prior experience, what would any measurable difference in IQ really mean? If we were to conclude that one species was superior or inferior to another, we would ultimately support the racist position since this would be a value judgment based on self-limiting Aristotelian logic. The question is not one of superiority or of inferiority but of adaptability.

A more holistic, ecological, or Zen conclusion would be that there are differences in intelligence as there are differences in other characteristics of behaviour, physiology, and structure. These differences represent evolutionary qualities that adapt a given species to a particular set of environmental factors which, in fact, fit it admirably to a specialized life-style. In man the evolving pattern of increasing complexity of the brain, coupled with increasing social complexity leading to increasing consciousness, must be seen as a continuum. In addition, the versatility of the species to adapt to new and different circumstances (i.e., a new set of environmental factors)—its flexibility—is a more meaningful question than its superiority to another species. This emphasis on superiority reflects the egocentric (or ethnocentric) way we tend to regard the world around us—the world of animals and of people from different cultures.

A genetically overspecialized animal and a culturally overspecialized person share the same limitations. Similarly an inbred strain of dogs and an inbred village of people or "aristocracy" may all reveal a higher incidence of genetic defects than more

A sheep dog pup with no prior experience with sheep, plays with a companion and shows many of the actions it will later use to herd sheep—an example of specialization and genetic selection. The pup turns, (A), drives (B), blocks (C), and ultimately stops (D), its playmate.

Photo: S. Halperin

Young chimp learning, through observation of an older companion, the tool-using behavior of "fishing" for termites with a stick.

Imitation and observational learning are the keys to culture. A wolf cub closely watches its mother and then imitates her.

randomly bred populations of mongrels and people alike. The phenomenon of hybrid vigor, where crossbred offspring acquire the best qualities of both parents, is evident. There is an analogy between the purebred dog and the human "specialist," with the mongrel and the human jack-of-all-trades and "Renaissance man," the latter being more adaptable in many ways than the former, less flexible genotypes and phenotypes.

Underlying the question of whether or not one species is more intelligent than another is the issue of reflective consciousness. The philosopher Descartes contended that man was different from animals in that man knows that he knows ("I think, therefore I am"), while animals simply know. They supposedly lack reflective consciousness. Recent studies of animal behaviour however, cast doubt on this speculative philosophy, and, in fact, the more we study animals the less clear-cut is the division between animal and man. Dogs and cats demonstrate insight and reasoning ability in certain learning tasks and also a capacity to learn from each other through imitation. Such observational learning, as when a mother cat takes her kittens out hunting, is perhaps the most rudimentary form of culture. Information can thus be passed on from one generation to the next. How the animal hunts, kills prey, and prepares a den may be instinctively programmed, and such innate tendencies form the basis for further learning. The young animal has to learn where, what, and when to hunt, where the best denning areas are, and so on. This he does by following and observing the parent or older members of the pack. Young wolf cubs may turn and flee at the first sight of a moose, and without the opportunity to observe parents or adult pack members hunt and kill, they might have little chance of survival. Wolves hunting together show strategy and sophisticated cooperation; two or three may lie in ambush while another drives the prey in their direction. We do not yet know how the wolves decide between themselves who is going to do what, or which role each wolf is to take in the hunt.

An awareness of self in relation to others is manifested in altruism, where one or more animals assist an injured companion, either guarding it or providing it with food. In less highly evolved

Reciprocal metacommunicative play-bow between dog and wolf: communication across 10,000 years of domestication.

animals like birds the infantile food-soliciting behaviour of an injured adult may automatically trigger or release care-giving behaviour in other birds. Such "regression" to a more infantile mode of behaviour and its potent releasing effect on other animals may be the primitive antecedent of what is generally regarded as altruism in man.

Shared awareness ("you know that I know that you know") must certainly be present in animals during play. For example, in playfighting, where all the actions of actual fighting occur, both animals know that the game is not serious. Very often a play-soliciting signal is given at the start that serves to set the mood and also conveys the animal's friendly intentions to its partner.

It seems clear then that animals do have some awareness of self, but we do not know how far this has developed in various species. Psychologists have shown that of the primates only chimpanzees will respond to a change in their reflection in a mirror, as when a white spot is put on their foreheads. They will use the mirror to groom themselves and to reach and touch marks they cannot see directly on their own bodies. Less highly evolved monkeys seem incapable of making the connection between a change in the mirror image (it has a white spot) and the fact that they now have a white spot on their forehead. But this is only one test of self-awareness, a special form of associative learning, and negative results in primates other than chimpanzees in no way prove that they lack reflective consciousness.

Chimpanzees have recently been taught to communicate by means of deaf and dumb sign language and to construct sentences using block symbols. They do indeed have a highly evolved learning ability, as well as an awareness of self (as demonstrated in the mirror studies), unlike other monkeys. Some believe, therefore, that the chimpanzee represents the "missing link" between man and other animals. If anything, it is a link in the continuum of increasing complexity/consciousness from animal to man; what is evident in human consciousness (such as awareness of self, altruism, insight, and reflective consciousness) must be present in some rudimentary form in other animals, varying in degree according to the complexity of the particular animal's brain.

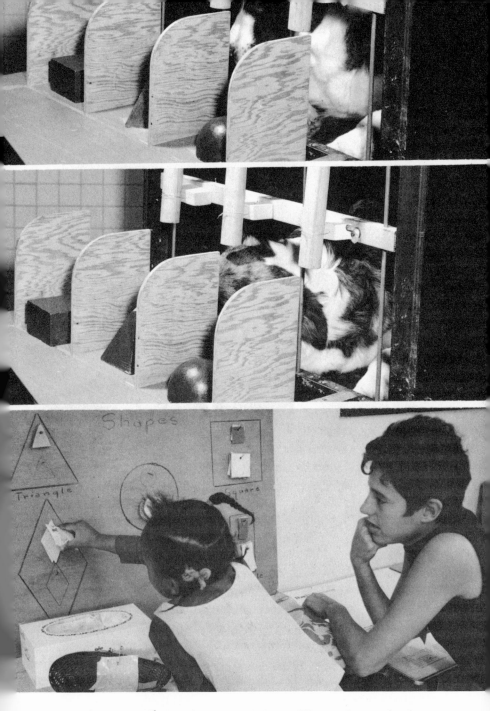

Dog and child learning to discriminate different shapes: the dog receives food reward but the child develops further, gaining verbal associations and abstract reasoning abilities.

Thus, while there may be absolute difference in intelligence between animal species, the differences are more on a continuum
of gradually increasing complexity/consciousness, with man separated more quantitatively than qualitatively. Man has evolved
such a degree of brain (and social) complexity that he has *more*
rather than a different *form* of consciousness than animal (although a qualitative change may occur once a sufficient degree
of complexity is attained). We must conclude, however, that
man's consciousness of consciousness—that inner "seeing" eye,
or reflective awareness—is not exclusively human, since a number of animal species *do* show insightful behaviour and the ability to reason.

In a verbal (written) test of mechanical aptitude a group of
black children scored miserably compared to their white American peers. Yet these same black children could strip down a car
in no time and, in fact, had a highly developed manual, rather
than verbal, mechanical aptitude. On the basis of the verbal test
alone the white students would seem superior; it is obviously important, therefore, to give tests (if they must be given) that control for specialized abilities in order to obtain a fair index of intelligence for different ethnic and socioeconomic groups of people
and different animal species alike. It is not surprising that people
from various cultures, adapted to widely differing physical and
social environments, should develop certain specialized sensory,
motor, and conceptual abilities. Absolute differences in intelligence, even if they were demonstrated, would really mean little.
Differences in specialization and in flexibility under different circumstances could tell us much more about the adaptability and
latent potential of a given animal species or race of people. In this
line of reasoning the teleological or holistic view, which, with a
different set of values and perceptions, is a more objective way of
seeing the world and of understanding other animals and people,
inevitably supplants the racist view.

The phenomena of racial differences, rather than racial superiority or inferiority and of individual differences (that can be more
within than between races), are great evolutionary assets. Individual differences provide a source of almost infinite adaptive forms.

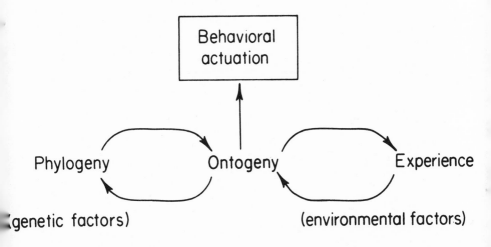

Behaviour, overtly expressed, is a product of both inherited characteristics (phylogeny) and experiences early in life, both of which influence development, or ontogeny, and the eventual behaviour phenotype. Neither genes (race) nor environment (culture) are the sole determinants of behaviour—the individual is a product of the interaction of both.

Without such differences evolution and adaptation to change would be crippled. At the genetic level uniforming would mean over-specialization; all the eggs *would* be in one basket, and the species would lack the flexibility to adapt to any sudden environmental change. At the cultural/social level uniformity, either conditioned in a Skinnerian utopia or enforced by traditional methods of conformity, is no less destructive to human growth. Unity of beliefs and higher values, not uniformity of thought and action, would be the foundation of a true global humanity characterized by diversity within unity, and in which the flower of genius is not crushed in a mass programming of uniformity and conformity.

Genes principally influence the direction of development for lower animals, while genes plus culture provide the directive forces for man.

Transcending the barriers of both racial and individual differences are two unitive similarities in the human psyche. The first is the "animal" level of basic needs (for food, companionship, sex, love, etc.); the second, that higher level is the reflective consciousness wherein the same beliefs and values have blossomed from the men of knowledge of all cultures throughout all of recorded history. The simplified schema (see figure) will help clarify these ultimate, yet basic, unitive similarities between people of all nations.

It is difficult to imagine that the needs and values at level B could ever unite different cultures. Global unity already exists at levels A and C—the feelings we all have for homeland, for our children, and those higher aspirations of religion and philosophy. Level B—the culture programming—tends to repress or sublimate level A and effectively blocks integration of level C into "everyday life." Each of us must strive in our own lives and for our children to overcome the overwhelming effects of level B—culture-programmed consciousness—so that humanity's full potential may be realized and expressed in a global sense of brotherhood. Freed from the ethnocentric filters that culturally ingrained expectations, values, and projections impose on reality, a man may see himself and others and appreciate them for what they

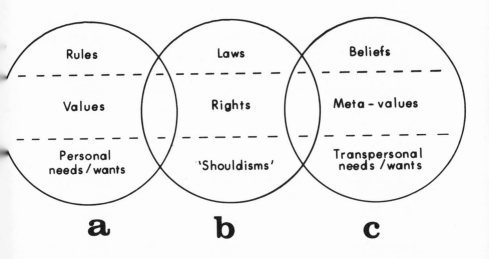

Rules	Laws	Beliefs
Values	Rights	Meta - values
Personal needs / wants	'Shouldisms'	Transpersonal needs / wants

a   **b**   **c**

At the levels of the instinctive (A), rational (B), and reflexive (C) minds, a different set of factors operate, creating separate conceptual realities and perceptual worlds alike.

are. "As a man is, so he sees," said William Blake more than a hundred fifty years ago. As it is, most of us have a false sense of unity via the social consensus of morality and values we share with others of our culture. Far more powerful are the unitive forces of love, understanding, and compassion that today, at best, we see only within the family and sometimes in small communities that can maintain some degree of freedom from outside cultural influences.

13

Levels of Consciousness:
Animal and Man

An animal like a dog clearly must have a sense of self and therefore an ego, together with the capacity for superego development since it is social. As in man, it also possesses an id, or "unconscious" realm of basic drives and feelings. Being social, the dog may manifest jealousy and guilt, as well as the need to conform, to be accepted, and to seek recognition and status. Man thinks he differs from animals in that only *he* possesses an ego, but the evidence would seem to deny that. Man, rather, has a more complex ego (and ego defense mechanisms) and a tremendous capacity for superego development—for acquiring the mores, values, and aspirations of his culture. Man also has a *super*-conscious, a fourth, higher, rational level of reflective awareness which, as far as we know, sets him in a very different conceptual world from other animals.

There is considerable loss of "body awareness" or id consciousness in the present educational system that emphasizes computer-like training of only the mind. Bodily sensations and social input and inner needs—feelings—are not often perceived, or only vaguely sensed. A fleeting feeling wells up and is stifled by a debate and judgment in the head—"Should I or shouldn't I?"

("Conscience doth make cowards of us all.") Conscience is consciousness at the rational level. Conscientiousness is the socially conditioned directing of one's energies for society. It can lead to obsessive-compulsive, non reflective (never pausing to look or ask why), antlike activity—a "busy" man preoccupied with the exaggerated importance of his own microcosm. He cannot laugh or step back and see himself and what he is doing objectively, and any disturbance seems to him a world crisis.

Awakening the superconscious frees man and enables him to rediscover his body and his feelings and to become alive. It not only repairs the mind-body split, it also brings man back not to his culture, which is relative, but to humanity. The superego *judges* right from wrong. Judge not others, and they will not judge you—then you will be a free man. The superconsciousness *evaluates* in relation to the body (feels okay or not okay), using experience and here and now feelings with which to evaluate and empathize.

Understanding of oneself and of others is then possible, while judgment selectively rejects or accepts others. It is not a question of accepting everyone, but with self-awareness comes self-acceptance, and it is easier then to accept and love others. Nothing is so strained as an egoideal—I *must* accept others and be accepted by them, and so on. With self-acceptance (self-love) the fear of not being accepted by others vanishes. If you really accept (know) yourself, it doesn't matter what others might do to you. "Know thyself." It is never possible until the superconscious is awakened.

In altered states of consciousness (as in meditation) various shifts in reality-perception, memories, and sensations occur, and glimpses of the superconscious may be experienced. With practice these may become firmly integrated and the nature of the ego significantly modified. With certain drugs, and especially in schizophrenic and psychotic states, a loss of ego rather than transcendence and reintegration of ego and superconscious may occur. This loss of self may be a terrifying experience—the limbo of living dead. Less extreme is the dissolution of ego defenses so that the person experiences an overwhelming flood of feelings that are sometimes tainted with paranoia.

The release from superego restraints, a "letting go," gives a sense of freedom and euphoria, but in its extreme form it leads to sociopathic actions. Fear of "letting go" because of fear of ego loss, of depersonalizing experience, of loss of self, can block the true "high" or mystical experience since contact with the superconscious is inhibited. Similar processes operate in preventing total orgasm. In full orgasm, the most commonly experienced "high," or altered state of consciousness, the id energies overwhelm the ego, and the "oceanic" reality of the superconscious is experienced for a fleeting moment: *diadic sartori* (to be "high" together). Comparable peak experiences of losing oneself also occur at odd times in every lifetime, sometimes when listening to a certain piece of music or walking alone in the country.

Sadly, many young people today use mind-altering drugs not always as an "escape" or for a mere thrill, but to experience the highest state of consciousness. Without proper grounding however, and the disciplined, patient work implicit in Yoga and other meditation, psychotic states may be precipitated. Without grounding, or establishing a center of self first, the "high" cannot be an integrated experience, and can ultimately lead to a "burned out," vegetative state like the chronic schizophrenic, or to delusional and illusory quasi-religious beliefs and practices. One should therefore "turn in" before "turning on," and be well grounded or centred in order to integrate new experiences instead of becoming lost in them.

We have and are something more than hands and brains, something more than sensations, feelings, ideas, and memories—that universal essence we all share in vague awareness and that we label soul or spirit. We reach it not in rational consciousness but through and above it. We feel it as joy and share it as love.

But what is all this doing, thinking, feeling, and sensing for? Science may ask the question "how" and probe into mechanisms and processes. Philosophy and religion may ask the question "why." Beginning with teleology, the "whys" are seen as evolutionary adaptations to survival and continuation of the species.

Yet still there are many "whys" to answer: Why is there life? What is its (or our) goal and purpose, or is it all an accident or a purposeless, cosmic coincidence or joke?

To ask why is extremely relevant to much of the human endeavor we see today, and it can jolt us out of habit, blind obedience, conformity, and ego striving. It is from the "why" rather than the "how" posture that values can be scrutinized. And the task of science today is to examine such value systems objectively and, hopefully, revitalize religion and philosophy in an ambience of social relevance and commitment.

Perhaps, after all our searching and questioning, the rational mind will rest, realizing that the thing in itself—life—is simply an expression of the essence of being. Also, there is no one answer, as there is no single goal or purpose.

All things are possible, and a multitude of personal values, goals, and purposes litter our past and future and confuse the present and the presence of that which transcends all time, space, and human striving. It is the one truth explicit in life itself—that emergent, all-suffusing essence of spirit (yet for most of us that is perhaps only experienced at the "transfiguring" moment of death).

It is from this truth that the expression, rather than purpose, of life takes preeminence over other earthbound endeavours. Expression, entailing feeling and experiencing or being, transcends the rational level of impression and doing. Metavalues associated with self-actualizing through expressive being replace the self-limiting values of goal-directed doing.

Technology can free us from this "doing" in order simply to survive and propagate, but it can trap us into more vain "doing" through habit formation and social conditioning. Spirit of place, of community, and of person is needed today to replace the sophisticated barbarism of enculturated materialism. We might begin by simply asking "why" and then by looking closely at the existential, moment-to-moment existence of animals, for the secret of life is there and not in our restless doing and ceaseless striving.

Nothing material endures, and ideas are no less ephemeral.

The only immortal thing humanity has to offer and can ever be a part of is love. It is an active, rather than passive, commitment to living in which universal love—the reverence for all life (self and others)—is an ethic transcending both the destructive forces on earth and the entropy of this universe. It embraces truth, compassion, humility, sympathy, peacefulness, and forgiveness. Love is the human term for that energy which rises above all others, and with it we assist in the creative process; empathy, compassion, and rational objectivism give meaning and fulfillment without which life is purposeless striving and suffering. Without it humanity has neither purpose nor direction. In its absence mankind suffers and creates more suffering. All other human endeavours, creations, and aspirations are but little lights that spark out and turn to dust across the endless continuum of space-time. Love is the energy that can unite humanity; it can reach across the terrible void between creation, death, and re-creation. It can be the single lifeline through the limbo of insanity between life and death— the void of the living dead. It is also the only force that can unify that which is within and that which is without—*Brahman* and *Atman*—and also bring together the spiritual or supraconscious and the realities of *everyday* consciousness.

But this energy, the spiritual homologue of the biological life force of the phenomenal world, can only flow freely when, like its physical homologue, water, it is pure (as truth). Since it is pure it will cleanse and ultimately be accepted by all who thirst, until they, too, are purified and free to give as well as receive. One must be able to love in spite of the rejection, mistrust, fear, and anger of others. Without love and without striving for its fulfillment, humanity has neither value, purpose, nor direction. In the absence or rejection of humane values (for others) and reverence for all life man is something less than human. He then abdicates the purpose of his own being and the fulfillment of his evolutionary destiny. Without love we live, consume, destroy, and kill in ignorance, as we will also die in ignorance. Faith transcends our skeptical and pessimistic view of the phenomenal world as one of competition, suffering, and destruction. The ethic of reverence for all life becomes an act of faith that makes us independent of those forces within the material world, so that we are free to act on them rather than be controlled by them.

We do not need to know all things and comprehend the nature of the physical universe in order to live fully. There is no end to the quest for knowledge, which, if we do not ask "why" and question our values, can lead us astray into the chaotic, incomprehensible, phenomenal world. But awareness simply is, and from this point in consciousness, through faith in one's ethic, one can see through the phenomenal world and become freed from it, rather than using it to give us the principles and directions for living. As Albert Schweitzer observed, "Reverence for life sets up a relationship between our minds and the universe that is independent of intellectual understanding."

14

The Three Stages of Man

Over the past million years all animals, with one exception, have remained virtually unchanged. That one exception, save for the few animal species that he has domesticated, is man. Rising on a wave of consciousness from a primordial past as a hairy *protohominid,* the phenomenon of man has touched every corner of this earth and is even now reaching to outer space.

From archaeological remains and from living "fossil" communities of primitive people today we know a good deal about our past. We were once a tribal species living in small bands or communities. Some were nomadic, others sedentary, and all had some form of leadership, rank order, or hierarchy and, of course, strong ties to one another through kinship and group allegiance. There were equally strong links to the land and to nature, which was their source of sustenance and hardship alike. Being born and raised in such a small tribal commune must have endowed people with a psychological makeup profoundly different from modern man's. Few of us today belong to a community or a tribe of relatives. Most have a nuclear family rather than an extended one living together in the same place. How does this affect us psychologically, since this change from a tribal and communal village way of life to nuclear family urban existence is a relatively recent evolutionary shift?

Life in the tribal community was highly personalized, each individual having a strong sense of belonging, acceptance, and identity. Pressures of conformity and fears of rejection and of being ostracized would be offset by one's deep socialization or attachment to the group. In fact, a *collective ego* must have been present—a group conscience and awareness. Only in such a group-oriented mind could voodoo operate, causing a person to die within twenty-four hours when a "curse" is placed on him by others or by a feared superior.

The collective ego of the tribe gave way to the superego conscience of the village community. "What will the Smiths and Joneses think?"—a separation of self from others in a less tightly socialized group—evolved. Next came the larger urban community with many people who never knew each other and who had many superficial acquaintances. "What will others think?" now became less personal, the superego a conglomerate of consensus values. The separation of self from others increased as the community became larger and more impersonal, if not depersonalizing. The "us and them" of "our tribe or village and those other neighboring tribes or communities" became internalized as the "us and them" within the socioeconomic hierarchy of the growing urban community.

The psychosocial effects of this generated the second stage of man, the *individuated ego,* where individualism replaced the collective personal ego of earlier times. A more impersonal urban environment, a less personal superego, gave rise to feelings of anonymity, depersonalization, and identity crisis. Ego defense mechanisms were elaborated as coping strategies since the need to belong—the deep need for sense of community and family—could not be satisfied by the nuclear family alone. The schism between self and others opened the door to more severe emotional disturbances, including schizophrenia and antisocial sociopathic behaviour, as well as to an increase in those disorders revealed in the first stage of community/tribal life. These include status striving, megalomania, depression and anxiety, guilt and para-

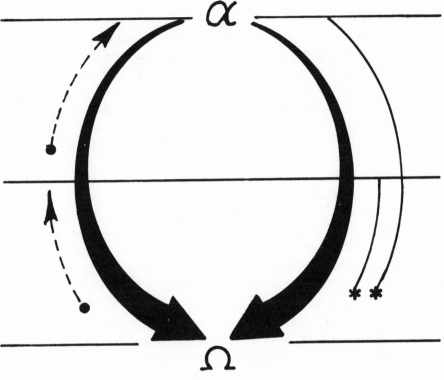

Schema of man evolving from alpha to omega, from (1) the tribal collective ego; (2) individuated contemporary ego; (3) collective global transpersonal ego. Avatars and teachers of insight have risen to level 3 today and in the past and inspire us towards this evolutionary destiny. With fear of losing personal freedom in the global state, some will turn back, as many today feel alienated in the highly individuated non-society of the technopolis and return to a tribal commune (indicated by broken lines).
From Fox (1974)

noia, and attention-seeking grooming ailments—neurotic conversion hysterias.

Perhaps the major advantage to this second stage in the evolution of human consciousness is that the individual did have more freedom beyond a collective ego and self-limiting world of a tightly knit community. It should be emphasized that human consciousness is a reflection of the culture and vice versa. In other words it is the society that determines much of the personality structure of its members, and they in turn constitute the society that guides, directs, and limits the potential of its children. The greater the flexibility, complexity, and diversity within the society, the greater will be the range and variety of individuals. With this comes a wider range of opportunity for self-expression and individual fulfillment for succeeding generations. But only up to a point. Complexity and diversity may reach a critical stage in which there is information overload and a breakdown in communications, which is the very fabric of society's structure. This, coupled with the rapid changes within half a decade in a "progressive" society, leads to identity crises, alienation, and what Alvin Toffler has termed "future shock." Stabilizing factors, in this case a sense of place, of belonging, and of community, are essential in any evolving system to temper the dynamic flux of change and growth. Without "freedom," or those factors whereby growth and change may occur within society and within the minds of individuals alike, stabilization causes stagnation. The society "freezes," becomes fossilized, and endures through generations without change, as in the Australian aborigines, or gradually decays, as in the great civilizations of Egypt and South India.

In this second stage in the evolution of consciousness and society priority is given to freedom of the individual, free enterprise, and competition, all of which contradict religious teachings of cooperation and brotherly love. Being progressive and therefore future-oriented, man is prone to a psychological misuse of time and of body energies. Instead of being in the here and now, he gets caught in the mind trap of planning and rehearsing—a trap that interferes with moment-to-moment feeling. Immediate experiencing is screened out by a mind focused not in the here and now but preoccupied instead with future plans and expectations. "Doing" takes priority over "being," and body energies are directed primarily toward future goals—accomplishment, success, status, and power. The individual becomes achievement-oriented and resembles a robot responding to a computer program. Add to this the fact that periods of nonstriving are not times for relaxation, but for stimulation to fill the void of boredom. The overstimulated brain in an information-charged environment suffers withdrawal like a morphine addict. "I'm bored," says the TV-nurtured child on his first day of camping, while his parents have camp chores to do to keep them preoccupied so that the pangs of stimulus-hunger are not felt. After a few days away from the information overload of the city, the nervous system *may* readjust, if given a chance, by not satisfying its stimulus-hunger in games, pastimes, and other distractions. (This stimulus-hunger may be aggravated by the fear of being alone.) From the "boredom" of withdrawal the addict may begin to turn in, instead of always being turned on by outside stimuli. For some this may be a "frightening void" experience since the inner spaces of consciousness are unfamiliar to them. For others such inner-directedness of reflective consciousness may spark creative inspirations and insights. For once the mind is freed from restraints and programming: The vacation was a positive experience. Energized and refreshed, the mind/body returns to the never ending routine of work, production, and consumption—to work in order to eat in order to work. Pleasure is mainly escape or diversion from this daily round, the *taedium vitae,* in the form of outside stimulation, e.g., vicarious sports, television, etc. The addiction—the stimulus-hunger—returns, an opiate for the anonymous masses who work and die for corporations which today are the new empires that are more powerful than nations.

Those who have other options—the affluent minority—are little better off, since they may be caught in the trap of materialism in which objects and property give them identity, security, and status. They hunger still for more because their lives, too, like the workers of the anthill, are also empty if there is no love for family or friends.

In the complex society of this second stage of human evolution, in which there is a great diversity of roles, what the individual does is, as we have seen, what he is. The performance principle of the work ethic gives the individual identity, without which there seems little purpose to living or to being. The measure of success is in accomplishment, and there is a startling resemblance of the individual to a machine. In fact, he is a part of the complex social machinery of the *technopolis*.

When the individual identifies wholly with his role, which is like a script or program plugged into a computer, consciousness is contracted and the full development of personality and potential alike is inhibited. Expectations of others tend to reinforce role play—the "professional image"—and since other areas of the self are not exposed, the character structure is like a mask or a hollow shell. Feelings, needs, and wants are neither experienced nor expressed fully. Interactions between people tend to be impersonal and superficial, lacking the depth and warmth of understanding and empathy that come from being in touch with one's own and another's wants and emotions. Such essentially human qualities may be inhibited through fear of rejection by others, who in turn remain closed and limit their interactions to self-fulfilling but self-limiting expectations and efficient, expedient rituals, clichés and pseudointimate conversational games and pastimes. The fear of rejection has many sources—from the deep feeling of aloneness and alienation to having to live up to others' expectations in terms of how one is perceived. In a complex society where there may be many daily interactions with people who are relative strangers, social and emotional distance may be maintained as an adaptation to crowding or interaction stress.

Living in large anonymous groups in this way dramatizes the experience of loneliness and alienation. But since others, too, experience these feelings and have the same deep, unfulfilled needs, there is a common ground where people *could* come together and experience closeness and belonging. Fear of intimacy, which is really a fear of rejection, however, keeps them apart unless a common crisis brings them together. Here more superficial needs may unite them in a common cause, which in turn provides a source of fulfillment for much deeper needs. A war, a rent strike, a boycott, or a factory slowdown may bring about a sense of unity and belonging that may endure long after the crisis has passed. Today ecocrises of pollution and shortages of food, raw materials, and fossil fuels may have a similar unitive effect on a highly fragmented and individuated society, as will the coming ice age. (Or conversely, such crises could lead to conflicts, power struggles, and war between the "haves" and the "have-nots.")

Perhaps this, or some other global crisis, may push humanity toward the third evolutionary stage of consciousness. The personal collective ego and the highly individuated ego of stages one and two respectively may become part of a supertribe, a worldwide brotherhood. Such a globally integrated community, made up of individuals whose consciousness rises above earlier evolutionary forms, would be *suprapersonal.* There would neither be loss of identity and personal freedom, as in the collective/tribal ego, nor fragmentation and alienation, as in the individuated egos of the technopolis. Instead, there would be personal freedom and belonging, unity with diversity as distinct from uniformity and conformity. In such a society the potential of succeeding generations would be more fully developed and expressed without loss of either unity or individuality. The balance between stability and flexibility would be maintained and expressed in the minds of the people and in the structure of the global community alike. In such a suprapersonal environment the dream of utopia today would be expressed in living and being. Consciousness and culture are one. Our children's children may indeed inherit the earth and attain this final evolutionary stage, which represents merely the end of the beginning.

15

The Other Side of
Communication and Consciousness

When the conversation in a room suddenly stops, the silence holds us and we are uneasy, embarrassed, and tense. Someone may crack a joke or shift his position, and we all relax at once. Did the sudden silence, so exquisitely synchronized between conversational groups of three or four, trigger an archetypal memory of danger? Do we now associate the uneasiness of social silence with some ill-defined danger, while the silence of the birds in the forest today is still a real indicator of danger? Crows are noisy creatures, and one leaving its group will give a call of departure, but if it flies off in silence, it is a warning to others of imminent danger.

Nervous, insecure people in groups either cling to the walls or corners and stay shyly silent or overcompensate and talk incessantly. Silence combined with aloneness can be intolerable, and yet compressed in that brief moment in a group, the tension of aloneness in silence is no less unbearable.

Habitual chattering, routine rituals, and the social games we all play tend to establish and maintain a given social distance. With sudden silence the spell is broken and we may really look and see each other for the first time. But this catches everyone off guard since it violates social conventions by implying greater attention and intimacy. To be looked at and seen can be a frightening experience. One who knows should avoid penetrating too immediately with the eyes in silence. A direct stare is intimidating and in all mammals can be interpreted at the instinctive level as a threat. Such unanticipated intimacy may be felt as an invasion of personal space—a dog will bark and withdraw; an infant may freeze or cry. Why can the eyes evoke such fear and apprehension? Where there is trust and love, the long gaze between lovers, mother and child, or faithful dog and master can lead subjectively to a merging of identity. The silent language of the eyes, and the deep energies it can evoke, is indeed a remarkable phenomenon.

Many people, especially those of "primitive" cultures, apprehend the twilight hour of dusk with anxiety or mystical reverence. The sudden silence of daytime creatures and that eternal moment of quietude before the nocturnal animals begin to sound, has an ominous foreboding more threatening than the roll of distant thunder. Poets and novelists of melancholic disposition see this time, associated with the setting (dying) of the sun, as a daily manifestation of one's own death to come, or as a warning of the inevitable (the end of the world or one's own death).

The silence of daytime creatures can be a warning of some imminent catastrophe—an earthquake, volcanic eruption, or a bushfire. Perhaps their sudden silence, triggered by an eclipse of the sun, gave this astronomical phenomenon more mystical significance than the eclipse itself to primitive people. Twilight at midday would be bearable without the terror of silence.

Since the beginning of recorded history, mystics have alluded to the inner silence that is the mirror in our consciousness of the outer silence our primate ancestors apprehended in fear and uncertainty. That inner silence when the internal dialogue ceases leaves consciousness aware of consciousness only. The void becomes a state of equipoise, a totality of being caught in an eternal moment, freed by the inner silence from both internal and external distractions. Some believe that without language there can be no consciousness, except for moment-to-moment experiences

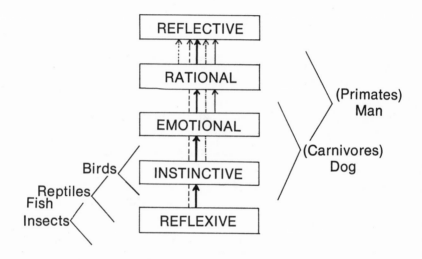

In the evolution of consciousness, the most highly evolved species carry with them some of the simpler qualities of more primitive forms: man's behaviour includes reflexive and instinctive levels of reacting, as well as rational and reflective thinking. This evolutionary pattern is also "recapitulated" in the development of the human infant.

and bodily sensations—an animallike state. But language, spoken or reflected internally, is often no more than noise, which is the verbal substrate of the rational mind. This part of the mind, which computes, abstracts, and predicts, binding time and experience in a nexus of expectations, is as self-limiting or self-fulfilling as the instinctive mind seeking gratification of basic needs and harmony of bodily sensations.

Through inner silence one may become liberated from the constant buzz and surge of the rational and instinctive parts of consciousness, and at the same time freed from the bombardment of external stimuli and projected expectations alike. A sunset, which no human endeavor can equal, may be held by the contemplative mind and experienced forever. It becomes something more than an external event or an esthetic sensation once the doors of perception are opened. Then the whole mind-body becomes part of that experience, the reflective or contemplative mind transcending the vital individuality of the rational and instinctive selves. The ensuing experience as oneness goes beyond words since this ineffable realm is not the verbal domain of the rational mind, which may label such as intuitive insights or creative inspirations—or sentimental subjective none-sense.

With silence one may attend. Only too often we hear but do not listen; we look but do not see. Habit—our set, "mature" ways of hearing and looking and relating—closes the door of perception (and conception). It marks childhood's end; the sense of wonder, arising from the newness of all things to the naive infant, gives way to familiarity and security (in the known world). A faceless, herdlike anonymity arises when such habits are part of consensus reality and are enforced through early socialization and education (brainwash) and coercive conformity (hogwash).

Sensory awakening can be accomplished in adulthood and that childlike sense of wonder reactivated. But it is difficult to change an adult's conditioned, enculturated way of perceiving and conceiving. One of the most effective ways is through learning to achieve inner silence. Outer silence—in a vow of silence or the nondirective silence of the leader or facilitator in an encounter group—can have a tremendous impact in breaking the habit of

constant noise. It also tends to enhance the quality of what is ultimately spoken. Silence is indeed golden, but to the rational mind
such a statement is illogical and the promises inherent in attaining
inner silence are illusory; outer silence may connote boredom, dis-
interest, laziness, or alienation. To the instinctual mind outer silence may mean danger, or at least generate unpleasant sensations
that are labelled variously as feelings of embarrassment, frustration, or rejection; inner silence means sleep or death.

To the contemplative mind, on the other hand, inner silence
is the totality of self that rises on the stillness of detached consciousness reflecting itself. Outer silence is no different from
inner silence, since what is without is an extension of what is
within. The totality of self includes all that is without, as well as
that which is within; perceiver and perceived are one and the
same at this level of consciousness.

Why, some may ask, should we, via silence or whatever other
means, wish to enter the third "house" of reflective or contemplative consciousness?* The instinctive mind may fear the void of
"needless" being and the rational mind may abhor the void of
"thoughtless" being. Thinking gets more in our way of being
than feeling—at least in this culture—because the feeling is repressed and thinking highly valued and rewarded. In fact the
thinking, rational, computer side of our consciousness is often
developed at the expense of all else. "Lose your mind and come
to your senses," said Fritz Perls—better to discover your mind
through your senses and at least integrate thinking and feeling.
Education today emphasizes the acquisition of cognitive skills
(develop the rational mind at all costs), while social skills (relating, cooperating, empathizing), aesthetic appreciation, and
sensory and body awareness are neglected. If we just educated
children's legs or right arms, we would all see the gross bodily
disequilibrium and asymmetry we had created. (Or would we, if
we thought it desirable and, by consensus, "normal"?) We do not

---

* "I think, therefore I am," said Descartes (but more correctly, "I think,
therefore I am a possibility" would be more appropriate at the level of rational consciousness). "I feel, therefore I am" is the instinctive level of consciousness. "I am, therefore I feel and think" is the more integrative metalogic
of reflective consciousness.

see so clearly the analogous, disproportionate development of just one part of the mind with which most present educational systems cripple our children. The tide and times are changing, however, since no one can live with this aspect of man's inhumanity to man. Social selection hopefully will insure that the present trend toward more integrative (humane) education will continue and gain greater momentum. Then, with a well-balanced mind/body and component parts thereof, man will be something more than a thinking penis. He will be able to discover the wonder of the world within and without, the world of the reflective mind without which no man is complete. He will not deny his thinking or repress his feeling, but rather he will actualize his potential *through* these attributes because they become balanced and integrated once reflective consciousness develops.

Most of us are more familiar with this third house of consciousness than we might realize. The ineffable, ecstatic experiences of lovemaking, of holding an infant, of beholding a sunset or a mountain, of merging with music, a game of golf, or football can be, in Abraham Maslow's terminology, "peak experiences." They represent a break from the routine of everyday doing and perceiving, where the essence of living and being is experienced as a state of oneness between perceiver and perceived or between action and reaction. One's individuality, personal needs, and expectations are transcended in a lucid moment of illumed being, of ineffable ecstasy. To deny this by rationalizing or by being afraid of losing one's identity, or by repressing all feeling or overdeveloping the intellect because of deep-rooted existential insecurity, is to deny the full expression and experience of being human. It is like tying the wings of a hawk—a man who cannot fly to the highest reaches of consciousness is something less than human. We must all learn to fly so that our children may reach beyond and explore the limits of human potential, since to be denied this freedom is to obstruct the very purpose of our being.

16

From Amoeba to Man

A phenomenon of the evolutionary process, which is hard to credit, is that certain characteristics present in earlier more primitive life forms tend to persist in more recent, advanced species. In a sense nothing is wasted in the evolutionary process. For example, the basic characteristics of the skeleton of a reptile are represented in the human skeletal structure. Similarly, the reptilian brain forms the core of man's complex central nervous system.

But reptiles are not the earliest life forms; the earliest, perhaps, are one-celled organisms like the amoeba. An amoeba consists of a nucleus and protoplasm—simplicity in itself. It can move freely in water by a flowing motion of the protoplasm and it can take on almost any shape. What qualities, if any, of the amoeba, one of the most primitive life forms, have persisted and can be demonstrated in man, the most highly evolved product of evolution on this planet?

Spontaneous motility—the free flowing of energy through the human body can be seen under certain conditions, and the resemblance to the protoplasmic contractions and expansions of an amoeba are striking. One of the first to recognize this was Wil-

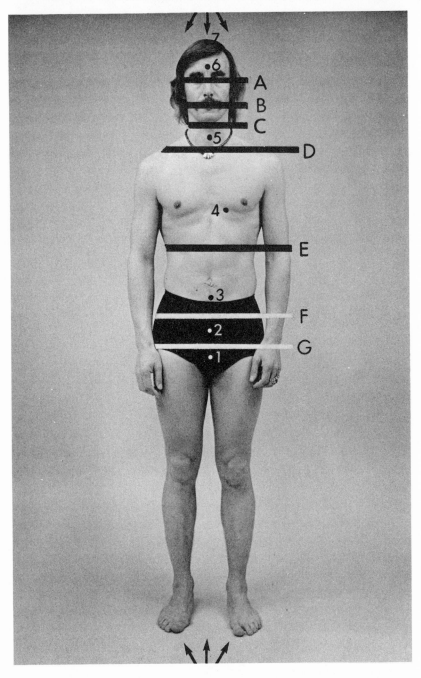

Horizontal bars (A-G) represent common segmental blockage of "tension" areas, and points 1-7 the approximate locations of the chakras or energy foci. Arrows above and below denote polar orienting energy fields of light and gravity.

helm Reich, who called the energy "orgone energy." During inspiration there is contraction, and on expiration, expansion. Energy waves can actually be seen coursing along the body to the fingertips and toes, especially when a person is lying down, relaxed, and engaging in deep abdominal breathing. In emotional states of tension, fear or anxiety, the flow of energy may be blocked in certain segments of the body. Chronic blocks—the "muscular armor" of Reich—may also be present as "rings of tension" that similarly block the flow of energy as well as drain it in order to maintain the tension. The areas of the eyes, jaw-mouth, throat-neck, shoulders, diaphragm and pelvis are the major segments where blocking occurs, and represent the somatic, or body sector, of psychic defense mechanisms and personality or character structure. Freeing a person from such mind/body blocks (via various therapeutic procedures) not only reenergizes the whole organism but also reinstates the polymorphous "free flowing" amoeboid state of freedom of feeling, expression, and movement.

Interestingly the "orgone energy" in a complex structure like the human body is organized into energy fields—the meridians and *Ki* points of acupuncture, and the *chakras* of yoga, with the centre around the umbilicus (the point of Hara of Oriental mind/body philosophy and medicine).

Unlike the amoeba, more complex organisms have evolved a nervous system that is like a diffuse net in primitive forms like the sea anemone, but which in the vertebrates becomes concentrated at the head or anterior end of the body. This process is called "encephalization." In man the anterior end, the brain, becomes a dual centre—one is the more primitive "visceral" brain associated with body sensations and feelings (being) and the other is concerned with "doing" (sensing and responding) and thinking. Because of our strong cultural emphasis on educating and using this latter centre, the centre of "doing" takes precedence over the centre of "being." A block in the flow of energy then develops, and the body is forsaken for a computerlike existence. Such a block may be visible in the eyes, jaw-mouth, or head-neck regions. Even sex may be an abstract experience, a

To train mind and body is education; to train the mind only is to rob the adult of half his true potential.
Photo: Herb Whitman

mere fulfillment of one of the body's needs, like eating or sleeping, "in order to keep it healthy." Every experience, if we are to live fully, however, should involve the *whole* organism—mind and body as one. Reich realized the significance of this as "total orgasm," hence the term "orgone energy" and the concept of polymorphous sensuality, which is experienced by a fully liberated and fully integrated mind/body. Ego defenses, ego ideals, and specialized doing or thinking can all work to prevent this unity, which is a childlike state, if you wish, but is experienced with the reflective consciousness of an adult.

The outward flowing of energy is analogous to the subjective experience of love, while withdrawal is associated with fear based upon a past pain or fear of rejection. Free-flowing energy is ease, as distinct from disease.

Sources of this energy are physical—food, air (*prana*), sunlight; psychic—ideas, thoughts, and feelings of one's own and others; and psychophysical—such as touch (physical-emotional contact with others). In Kundalini yoga, which deals with freeing the flow of energy through the body (the "serpent power"), additional sources of energy are thought to come from below (the earth) and from above (the spiritual "halo"). Certainly the earth provides the gravity force that influences the alignment and functions of our body energies, and to this we should add the energy fields of others that also affect our orientation and functions (or direction and expression of feeling and actions).

The Christ symbol of the exposed heart represents the fourth level of awareness and opening of the fourth chakra which is associated with love and empathy. Higher chakra, or keys to higher levels of mind/body integration and awareness, include those located in the throat (communication), between the eyes (knowledge), and on the crown of the head (Christ or cosmic consciousness—the "halo" of the saints). Chakras below the fourth one include the abdominal region below the navel (power), the genitals (sexuality), and the base of the spine (grounding, the seat of Kundalini, the root of reality-contact). Activation of the latter is a key point in Alexander Lowen's Bioenergetic Therapy in emotionally disturbed people in order to get them

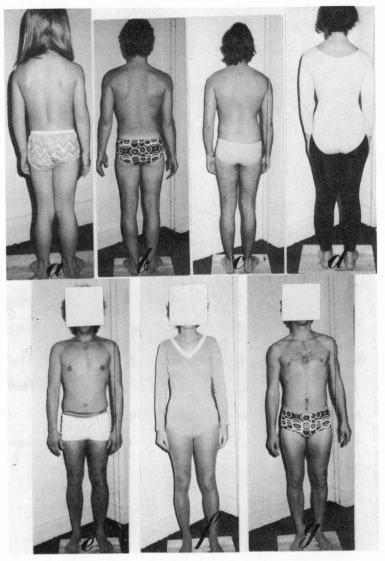

Congenital overdevelopment of muscles on right side (a), an unusual anomaly, more commonly acquired as in right shoulder region of (c). Excessive retraction of shoulders with twisting (scoliosis) and arching of lower back (b), right shoulder dropped, and imbalance of weight on right leg (d), raised shoulders and overinflated chest (e), standing on right leg (f), and dropped right shoulder and excess weight on right leg (g) are gross assymetries which can indicate earlier physical/psychological trauma, current emotional tensions, and future, more serious complications, since structure influences function and function will be even more severely affected.

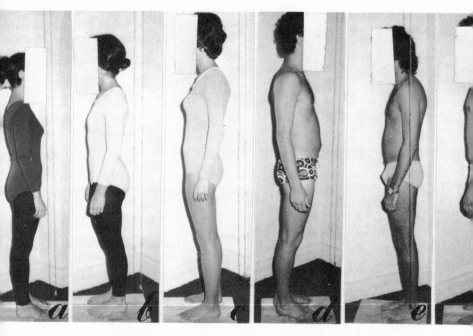

Few people stand and move with optimal balance and unstable equilibrium. Knees locked (a), head thrown forwards, shoulders pulled back, and weight misplaced forwards (b, c & d); severe misalignment of head with shoulder 'humping' (e); and tense raised shoulders and overinflated chest (f)—interfere with natural functioning and feeling and will cause severe problems later in life.

to literally "stand on their own two feet." Most western people operate on chakra levels two and three—sexuality and power/control being interrelated primary occupations. Energy is focused principally in these two psychophysical centres at the expense of other higher ones. Since these are rarely activated, they are consequently never fully integrated into the total mind/body affective-effective schema. A knowledge of these energy-related phenomena is important to our understanding of human behaviour, health, and disease. Although such knowledge derived from Eastern philosophy and medicine is alien to our Occidental training and thinking, we would do well to investigate, evaluate, and integrate some of this wisdom of the ages, which is no less than the wisdom of the body itself.

A careful analysis of a person's body—of posture, muscle development, idiosyncratic attitudes and movements, breathing patterns, and expressive actions or emotional displays and mannerisms—can be extremely revealing. Much is unconscious to the person, so that a deeper awareness of the body naturally leads to a better integration of mind and body. Indeed, psychoanalysis without work on the body is of limited value since a person is both mind and body.

Sometimes after an intensive massage treatment my patients experience a tremendous release of energy that has been blocked in one or more of the body segments (see Figure 1). Occasionally they also experience recall of some earlier psychological or physical trauma, and a flood of feelings may surface.

A useful exercise is to tense every muscle in the body and then relax, followed by the assumption of some exaggerated posture (display) associated with one emotion—fear, assertiveness, or anger. The body posture may trigger genuine feelings and help get the person in touch with his body or the somatic side of his psyche.

So often I find that people have a certain personality or character structure (and role or mask) that is, in part, mirrored in the body. And the body habits, armouring, and attitudes are deeply ingrained, automatic, and unconscious, though they "feel" normal. Making a person conscious of these, and of his breathing

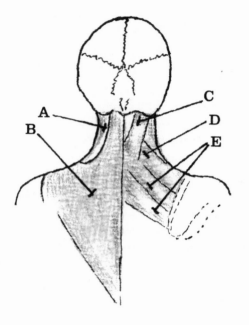

    The "body armor" neck tension, headache, raised-shoulder region. Muscles involved, which will respond to massage and especially to Rolfing or Alexander head realignment, include (A) sternocleidomastoid, (B) trapezius, (C) splenius capitis, (D) levator scapulae, (E & F) superior and inferior rhomboid muscles.

The shoulder-raised threat display of many primates including man is clearly shown by this chimpanzee, whose display makes his head virtually disappear. In man, such a display may become "frozen" in a more permanent attitude of defiance or assertiveness.

Photo: S. Halperin

Body Region	Muscles	Symptoms/Behaviour (Characterology)
Eye	orbicularis and retractor oculi, frontalis	Eyes hidden—fear, withdrawal; chronic eye tension.
Nose	levator nasolabialis	"Flared" anger.
Forehead	frontalis	Surprise; chronic frown.
Jaw-chin	masseters, buccinators, mentalis	Bite inhibition ("displacement" gum chewing and "redirected" tooth grinding); assertive protrusion; slack "idiot"; fear/submissive retraction.
Mouth	orbicularis oris	Tight, closed-bite inhibition; aggressive pucker.
Neck-throat	sternocleidomastoid, platysma, deep laryngeal	Tight-blocked communication; inhibited crying; swallowing tension; (gag-reflex-vomiting releases tension).
Head-neck	sternocleidomastoid, splenius capitis, semispinalis capitis	Upward tilt—superior; bow—inferior. Misalignment—tension, headache. Alexander integration point.
Shoulders	levator scapulae, rhomboids, trapezius (often overdeveloped)	Raised—tension, fear, anxiety; startle reflex.
Upper Back (scapulae)	rhomboids, infraspinatus, teres major and minor, deltoids (often overdeveloped)	Inhibited striking or reaching: withdrawal or contracted, chest out, and assertive/offensive.
Buttocks	gluteals, anal sphincter	"Tight ass" defensive, rigid conformist (may involve adductors of legs—outward rotation of feet, flat feet); tension, hemorrhoids. Flaccidity with inward rotation of feet.
Legs	various muscle groups	Overdeveloped-inhibited flight (gastrocnemius); "weak knees"—fear submissive—(contracted biceps femoris); hyperextended (locked knee stance) with head-neck and pelvis misalignment (flabby hyperextended flexors, shortened quadriceps and rectus femoris). Foot misalignment—knee cartilage problems.

Important to note relations (proportions) between these different body regions for over- or underdevelopment, flaccidity, adiposity, and asymmetries between right and left sides.

Body Region	Muscles	Symptoms/Behaviour (Characterology)
Chest	pectorals, intercostals	Expanded—aggressive/assertive or defensive/fearful. Collapsed in passive, submissive, and defensive/depressive.
Arms	linked with energy flow/block from shoulder and upper-back regions	Weak, withdrawal; cold hands (poor circulation). Excessive musculature with need to control (i.e., insecurity), or anger (fist clenching).
Back (trunk)	longissimus dorsi, latissimus dorsi, spinal erectors, etc. (shortened with pelvic tilt)	Inflexibility—"straight back" of discipline, conformity. Curvature (scoliosis) with overdevelopment of one side (right side achievement). Lordosis—upper back hump and lower back hollowed with head-neck misalignment—headache, lower-back pain.
Lower Back pelvis	iliocostalis lumborum, quadratus lumborum, iliopsoas	Forward tilt of pelvis—lower-back pain, "genital withdrawal," sexual problems. Sacrum "key" of Rolfing technique.
Abdomen	rectus abdominis, internal and external abdominal oblique: diaphragm link with chest for deep breathing—"release" to ease tension	Low tone in "infantile" potbelly —poor self-control. High tone in defensive armouring, "ticklish" defensiveness; seat of tension, "butterflies."

Note: An animal uses certain muscles to display fear, threat, submission, etc.); then it relaxes. Man may chronically manifest these attitudes (in mind and body), i.e., "frozen" displays, or body character formation. Other abnormal postures are often simply "bad habits."

patterns in different social/emotional contexts, is one of the most potent and effective ways of generating self-awareness and of freeing blocked potential for growth, expression, and experience —for living in a fuller and deeper way.

Jogging, Canadian Air Force exercises, Mr. Atlas body-building, and so on are good for circulation and muscle tone, but only too often more muscle is built around a poorly integrated frame. This sort of exercise is a waste of time in the long run, but such compulsive, disciplinary regimens are attractive to the rational (robot) mind. Sadly, here, as in other activities, the performance principle (and work ethic) can take precedence over the pleasure principle (feeling and experiencing). The natural sensuality and sensitivity of the body are lost in mechanical proficiency, strength, and stamina.

Stanley Keleman, a renowned West Coast body therapist, emphasizes that many parts of the body (like the mind) may be repressed and developmentally retarded. He states that "The flow of life does not mean discharge. Discharge is not the goal, expression is; knowing is not the goal, experiencing and self-forming is. Sexuality does not simply mean genital interplay, it means the development and expression of the whole person in contact with his universe. We have never been taught that our world develops as our feelings develop." He shares Teilhard de Chardin's belief that the deepening and developing of love (for self and others, which is a fundamental blossoming of awareness) is man's uniqueness and responsibility in the universe. Without ease and awareness there is disease and ignorance, and a life of frustrated and inhibited growth and suffering seems inevitable. Moshe Feldenkrais, the Israeli body therapist, contends that once a person becomes aware of his total mind-body habits and reactions, the road to personal fulfillment is opened. Such body therapies are regarded with some skepticism by our conservative medical practitioners, who are lost in their depersonalizing institutions and seem to know more about disease and less about health and normality than they should. We need to learn more about the whole mind-body and human behaviour in sickness and health. An awareness of our own body reactions, breathing pat-

Students explore feeling and emotional expression through movement: body awareness is developing in this modern dance class.

terns, postures, habits, and attitudes is perhaps the most important educational priority today, since education generally neglects
all but the rational computer part of our mind-body gestalt. We
must therefore develop the natural animal within us which is
culturally repressed in order to be fully alive and human.

17

The End of Dreams:
Man Is Animal and God

As early pioneers, you, America, fought and mastered the wilderness and "won" the West. Or did you? You destroyed nature to feed your greed in a dream of progress. Yesterday you fought to master the world and you lost. You destroyed cultures and fed communism with your fear. Today you fight to master space, but will you? Is it not an escape—a distraction from the reality of your earthworn space?

Begin again—the journey into the inner space of your own culture, your own minds, values, traditions, fears, and hopes. After that you may have the wisdom and humility to forge a global passport when you learn that you and others of different cultures are of one nation and one spirit. Then you will have the credentials to journey to the further reaches of the mind and the universe alike.

The imprint that you have left on nature and on other nations would be no less destructive to other worlds you might reach. Do not continue to violate my dreams or the serene unity of the stars. First discover the music of the spheres in the wilderness and in alien voices from distant lands. You will not lose your minds to the music of the spheres or your identity or cherished values by subtly merging with other cultures. You will, instead, find greater riches and discover the freedom and joy of no longer being culture-bound and value-limited so that you can only perceive and judge others through your own narrow set of values and beliefs.

Culture-bound, you will never be able to fully explore inner *or* outer space. The world, yourself, and the universe will continue to be mysteries. How can you rest now, knowing so much about so little and being aware of nothing except the knowledge that blinds you to other realities and comforts you from the fear of the unknown? The rational mind destroys myths and fills the void of knowledge and awareness so there are no mysteries. The child dies in the man, and the man sleeps.

The child's polymorphous potentiality is destroyed so that the man, the culture-programmed "robot," can efficiently serve society. Like an ant which inherits instincts to serve its colony, so the man is imprinted with a similar set of rules, and his capacity for such programming is no less innate.

The natural child is the catalyst to creativity—curiosity and wonder being its key characteristics. Alive and functioning in the adult, the natural child integrates with the "robot" and allows a person to transcend his cultural destiny, discovering higher consciousness in creative and reflective awareness. The superconscious or overmind develops: The "starchild" of inner space and the true explorer of outer space. This is very different from a military NASA robot, who utters inarticulate monosyllables or repeats trite quotations when his conditioned mind implodes with the rush of feelings at seeing himself outside earth. (But even he may return to earth after such an experience and be a different man—his inner child reborn!)

You and I react and feel like animals, but unlike them we also think and reflect. If we deny our spontaneous reactions and feelings, we are less than animal, for, after all, we are only animals that think more than others.

Feelings and reflective consciousness can be integrated in moments of poetic inspiration and creative insight when the mind seems to penetrate the barrier of objective perception and

subjectively unifies the perceiver and the perceived. The follow-
ing lines, written during a field trip to India, illustrate this point.
It is perhaps no coincidence that the passage echoes both Loren
Eiseley in *The Immense Journey* and Henry David Thoreau in
Walden, both of whom spent much time resonating with nature
in this ecstatic state of consciousness.

I feel my permanence in the rooted tree and my tran-
science in the wind-torn leaf. I sense the timelessness in
the rhythm of days and seasons and the movement of
the butterfly. I see the enormity of the wilderness and
the galaxies above, and the microcosms, no less important to the ant under its fallen tree. Nothing is more
or less significant or important than anything else; no
place, individual, or event. All is one, converging in
harmony, diverging in a multitude of individuals of
infinite variety: As under the stone, so it is on earth
and in the heavens. A forest of many trees, all different; a dawn chorus of birds, each subtly unique but
united in time and space. A crowd of people and you.
And you and me; and I and thou.

Where is this oneness in the world of commerce and
technology, except between the man and his organization and between the producer and the consumer?
Product and user become one. Here is a oneness, har-
moniously combining individuality (in the custom-made
product), diversity (many brands to chose from), and
unity (conformity of values and needs). The material
world thus easily replaces the world of nature for
many, and they lack nothing except that essence which
we call spirit or soul. They feel the spiritual hunger
that no human product can satisfy as an inner emptiness. They seek and consume and acquire more, but
this inner feeling can never be satisfied by material
things. Only in the silence of the mountain pines, in
the vibrant sounds of earth as dawn breaks over the
jungle, or in the cold ice of the Arctic tundra may

a man find food for his soul, which few men and no man-made product can provide. When a man returns to nature, to the hard boulders, the stones, and smooth pebbles, the warm rocks, the ocean-glacier-river-mountain, tundra-forest-jungle-desert of his senses, his eyes, ears, and nostrils are filled with all that is there, and even through the soles of his feet and his fingertips he experiences. The imperceptible wholeness, continuity, and oneness of all things is perceived when all sensations and senses converge within and without. The magnitude of the All is felt, experienced: One becomes both the experience and the perceiver. This is the nature of man and the threshold of his earthly potential from which he may grow, freed from his cultural programming, beliefs, values, and expectations. Without nature a man will not know himself or cross the threshold that closes him to new realities. Locked in to the safe, predictable reality of every day, he shares a consensus reality of others, and the culture-prison of the senses is enjoyed, for no other way is conceivable.

In the jungle I felt a oneness with all things and at the same time my awareness of myself gave me a sense of separateness from those things. Perhaps this is the essential quality or state of being human, for we are neither completely animal nor god or spirit, separately.

If this is so, then no man can respect himself if he does not respect nature. Nor can a man love his neighbor if he does not see the trees and animals as his brothers as well.

An act of violence against nature should be judged as severely as that against society or another person. The turning over of a stone, the unnecessary felling of a tree, or the slaughter of an animal is a crime to be weighed in judgment against the wants and needs of the person and the values of his society. A fair judge could not come from his society. Must nature judge in the end, giving man a barren wilderness for his children's children?

Societal values of peace, harmony, and progress, and of production, competition, and profit are contradictory. For a poor man heaven is a full stomach, and for one with food heaven is a drive in a new car. For many, though, more wealth and power may be the life goals, while the simple pleasures of others who walk in quiet woods or along sunlit shores are meaningless.

Awareness of nature and its message is synonymous with enlightenment. An act of conservation is an affirmation of that awareness. Without nature the essential quality that makes us human would be lost. No machine, corporation, or other social or architectural edifice can inspire and awaken the human spirit in the same way. If it does, then we may become trapped into worshipping ourselves, the false gods of our creations, surrendering our humanity to the machine or the "system."

Mass-produced impersonal items and luxury products alike, made not with the spirit of the craftsman but stamped with a serial number by a faceless machine, reflect the depersonalization of a consumer society. The products and the dependent materialists alike are akin to robot animals in a plastic jungle.

Flames of greed, fanned by the winds of progress, consume and pollute the West. Hunger gnaws the silken loins of the East, where beggars moan for bread and claw through the garbage of the affluent. The rich look to the West as a model of their dreams and rarely see through the illusion. Likewise, many in the West see the East as a spiritual cornucopia and seek outside what they can only discover within themselves.

Man is both animal and god in terms of feelings and awareness, but in a sense he is neither: He is caught between the two extremes of his being. This essential duality of human nature is our present and perhaps transient condition as an evolving and changing being. It sets us apart from our animal brothers and from the ineffable, which in moments of great clarity we intuitively feel within and beyond us.

Such a duality of man represents a split or schizophrenia in his nature. It can create a "tension" between deeper feelings and needs and the higher reflective consciousness (i.e., the *superconscious* or man's awareness of his awareness).

Primitive (Biotic) Man

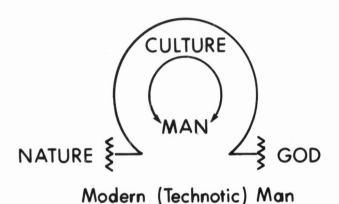

Modern (Technotic) Man

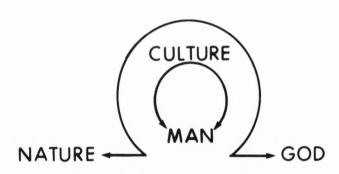

Future (Noötic) Man

Modern man must endeavor to integrate himself again with nature and god (implied not as personifications but states of awareness), since culture today separates and alienates us from both.

Does this mean that all members of our species are sick? Not entirely. Tension or inner stress can be a positive stimulus to growth and evolution, but not for all individuals. Some may be overstressed and may ultimately breakdown physically and emotionally. The schizophrenics in our mental hospitals are evidence of such breakdown in more susceptible individuals who are unable to adapt, to resolve the inner tensions and outer conflicts of different realities and states of being. Yet others seem to thrive in the same environment.

But the majority neither flourish nor withdraw into schizophrenia—nor do they live and grow or withdraw and vegetate in living death. They are in limbo, caught in the no-man's-land between animal and god. This void is filled by a man-made world of ideas and values that creates a very special reality for those who are a part of it. We call it civilization, a composite of moral and ideological constructs and traditions handed down from one generation to the next. It can be a vital link connecting and integrating the two poles of our nature. But it can also be a trap in which we are held in limbo, out of touch with these other realities of animal and god.

Man is a cultural being; at birth his brain is already developed with expectations that further programming will be received from others, from the culture. This capacity to acquire the information of a whole civilization is inherited. It is an attribute transcending the limited amount of information that can be transmitted in the genes from parents to offspring. And yet the capacity is no less inherited!

Nonhuman primates such as chimpanzees and baboons and carnivores such as the wolf have a lesser capacity to hand on "traditions" from one generation to the next. The development of this capacity is greatest in our own species and sets us apart from even our closest animal relatives. Where less evolved animals depend on instinctive, inherited capabilities, the more evolved ones come to rely more on each other up to the point

reached in man, where a newborn child is almost entirely culturally (or environment) dependent.

As the brain becomes more complex, the more conscious is
the animal that possesses such a brain. It has been said that an
animal like a wolf or dog "knows," but man "knows that he
knows." This implies that, with continued evolution, the brain
becomes more complex and more conscious—and then a great
leap forward occurs when a critical stage of complexity is attained. At this stage the mind is reflective; it sees itself—one is
conscious of consciousness.

So far as we know from scientific research, the supraconscious
or reflective awareness is present in more evolved animals like
dogs and chimpanzees, but is virtually dormant in these species
compared to its development in man. We see this level of consciousness developing gradually in the human infant as its ego
begins to differentiate and individuate from its earlier postnatal
symbiotic attachment or union with the mother. Impaired ego
development can not only distort reflective consciousness (self-
awareness) but also severely limit the development and actualization of human potential.

Given, therefore, a remarkable brain and a cultural heritage,
man is clearly very different from other animals. The pattern of
evolution is not a direct linear progression from simple nervous
system to computerlike brains of increasing complexity. There is
also increasing social complexity from which culture emerges.
Consider the social complexity of a termite city or a beehive, in
many ways analogous to our own. Evolution in the insect world
took a different turn—brain complexity changed little, but social
complexity in some species continued to evolve. In man these
two axes—neural and social complexity—tend to be more interwoven and evolved at comparable rates. Our brain development,
however, began to lag several thousand years ago, and in contemporary man there is now a schism between brain and cultural
evolution, the latter changing at an incredible rate within one
generation. Many writers have emphasized that this schism can
create havoc for many people who try to adapt to rapid external
changes, and that these stresses of "future shock" add further to

the burden of being human. It is a burden for many, a critical source of stress like the inner tensions described earlier that may lead to mental breakdown. For others, stress is a challenge, a motivating force without which life would be bland, if not pointless.

Are these different ways of reacting an indication of natural selection operating, where only the most adaptable—the "fittest" —succeed?

Is it imperative to adapt and strive for success, or are there alternatives open for those who do not wish to be swept up in this accelerating spiral of human "progress"? Is this natural evolution, or has something gotten out of hand? Are the culture-spawned values of progress and change the catalysts that can destroy the essence of humanity and the delicate fabric of our cultures? Are those who are able to survive, adapt, and succeed the social mutants of a new depersonalized, materialistic species of the near future—*Homo technos,* the faceless, anonymous robots of corporate empires who worship their own creations (like the false gods of the Bible) and whose minds, souls, and identities are sold to the system (the devil of the Bible) that controls and rewards them? Are these the ants of the future whose brains will cease to develop, but whose prosthetically aided bodies and chemically or electronically regulated minds will be kept functioning—functioning to serve a society so complex it is run entirely by computers?

One Zen master commented that he sees Americans generally as being too achievement-oriented; they see and act rather than feel, and find doing more important than being. So, paradoxically, we fight for peace and strive for perfection (nonstriving equipoise). The ego seeks mastery, success, and power, and is the trap of *Tai chi,* karate, meditation, and other "growth" pursuits —rather than the self perceiving the process instead of the finished product as being the whole point of the exercise and of life itself. The ego-image seeks the illusory goal of perfection instead. If there is perfection, then there must be imperfection, and the mind works in making often unreal and self-limiting comparisons and judgments. As Seikas Hasegana observed in the Washington *Post,* when Western society learns to see goodness and badness as part of the same thing, then it will be all right. He states that "Achievement and achieved change are illusory. The beauty is there already, just as Americans have Zen in their lives—yet they go out seeking it."

Is work the only thing modern man can do? Is there no alternative way of living? The motivation seems not to be primarily for money, for financial security. A rich man will *still* work—will even kill himself with a coronary by overworking. This obsessive compulsion to work is programmed into the robot in infancy: The deeply ingrained Judeo-Christian ethic of work for rewards—security, success, status, and power.

If one has security in and of oneself and needs neither success nor power, what then? Can such a person "work" in such a value system anymore? Many of these are the dropouts of today who are discovering new life-styles and enjoying what others cannot even feel or perceive as worthwhile or pleasurable.

But what of tomorrow if our society were to give us all equality and security, eliminating the need to work for security, success, status, and power? What of the man who works only two days a week and another who retires at forty? What can the mind and body, trained only for work, do when there is no work? Boredom, apathy, depression, feelings of worthlessness and purposelessness set in. Suicide. Drug therapy. Stimulus-hunger is only partially satisfied by mass entertainment, sports, drinking, drug and sex parties, and vacationland weekend resorts. Encounter and sensitivity groups may help some. Programmed for work but not for play, these discarded robots can only partially realize the pleasure principle.

Work may become a privilege for a chosen few, while many will take jobs simply to keep themselves active and free from boredom. Inactivity and boredom could lead to total breakdown of a nervous system that has become wholly dependent on varied input from the environment. Stimulus-hunger would be satisfied by psychedelic drugs and visual and auditory input in the form of television and movie entertainment. Alcohol and tranquilizers would deaden the stresses of routine and boredom and relieve the interaction stress of crowded urban environments. Stimulants would counteract these drugs and heighten the sensory pleasures associated with entertainment and sex. This is not the blueprint of a society of the future. It is society today. Perhaps tomorrow a man may not need to work in order to keep his mind and body healthy. Today he must, and if he loses his meaningful job, or if he suddenly discovers the work he does is meaningless, he will fall sick or rapidly become senile. He may even die.

He hopes education in the broadest sense will save his children from his fate. Education of more than the rational bio-computer—of the body, the senses, feelings, and higher consciousness—would produce more complete, healthier, and more humane beings. They would not suffer from boredom or seek varied stimulation as an escape or anesthetizing syrup for unemployed minds and unoccupied senses. They would be able to relax, do nothing, and enjoy it, not feeling deprived, guilty, or anxious, and not experiencing rushes of energy when they didn't need it. Being and living would be more important than doing and working, and their minds and bodies would be able to adjust more easily to varied levels of stimulation and physical activity. With bodies supple and alive and minds flexible and creative, they would be able to enjoy fully the pleasure principle. Their minds and bodies would not be crippled or distorted through programming for "specialist" tasks, but rather have a polymorphous potential—to be anything and to do anything. And this would characterize adulthood, not just infancy. We see this same polymorphous potential—supple bodies and curious and creative minds in our children today—but few escape being crippled and most lose the potential in being moulded by society. What happens to them? Shaped in mind and body, they are conditioned to conform to prescribed roles. In the same way hormones from the queen termite control the brains and bodies of infant termites and direct their development for the "benefit of society."

Society would be richer if all adults retained and developed potential that is revealed earlier in life. It is a false premise that teaches man he must give something up or sacrifice for the "benefit of society," which means for the benefit of others. For these "others" are no less crippled than you and me!

Is this not what that political radical preacher, Jesus Christ, was attacking when he said, "Ye must first become as little children before ye can enter the Kingdom of Heaven"? He wanted humanity to be free to be and to become—to actualize its potential. Step out of the cultural mould, get mind and body whole and together again, reintegrate the polarities of our nature— *animal and god.* Without this wholeness a person has no soul and society lacks the spirit of humanity, that essence which is embodied in the child, in Christ-consciousness, and in this promise of heaven—a heaven on earth, here and now, is possible. The Buddha, too, said that heaven (*nirvana*) is on earth (*samsara*) for all those who can feel, see, and know.

Will those whose minds and bodies refuse to adapt today or tomorrow be the extinct dinosaurs of the near future? Or will they annex themselves from the technophiles and live like a separate species, not yielding to the material riches of the "other world" but seeking instead the inner riches of a more grounded and spiritual life, living in a smaller personalized community close to the more tangible and fulfilling reality of nature?

Many people of all ages are doing just this today. I am not, then, talking about the future but about the here and now. We must all pause for a moment—a difficult feat when we are so caught up in that accelerating spiral of progress and change— and look. Look and see with clarity, an even more difficult feat when our very nervous systems, perceptions, and values are programmed for the one reality in which we are caught. And when we really see where we are now, and where we are going with our lives, and think of our children's children, we may have the clarity of perception and the courage to decide and choose what we really want—want, as distinct from what others say we *should* want, or what our own neuroses, ego defenses, and egocentric needs make us *think* we want.

This incredibly difficult but vital step must be taken if we are to grow, to realize our potential, and live a full life in every sense. Just as the infant has to separate its identity (ego) from its mother, so the adolescent (or adult) has to separate himself from his culture (superego) in order to find his own center of self. It is from this center that we feel, think, and grow. Without contact with and individuation of this center from mother and culture, the individual has the identity and self-awareness of an ant. He cannot know if his feelings, needs, wants, and ideas come from himself or from others. He cannot know how much his behaviour—his whole being—is controlled by others and by his own conformity to a consensus reality that others in the same state as he blindly fabricate.

This vital step does not involve a radical rejection either of mother or culture, but a stepping back and away in order to pause, look, see, reflect, and act. It may be interpreted as rejection, as unloving, as radical political or social deviancy: The infant rebels and cries no, and the adolescent struggles to find identity by being a nonconformist. Parents, teachers, and others feel unloved, rejected, and even threatened, and the growing human being may be crushed into conformity by devious threats and conditional rewards and, worse, by the instillation of guilt in his consciousness. Love becomes conditional to the infant; life becomes conditional to the adult; conditional upon fulfilling the needs and wants of others who have not discovered their own centres, and who therefore do not really know what they need or want. The child becomes a human ant, other-directed rather than inner-directed.

Many parents and educators alike are aware of these facts today, but few are able to do much about it because they have not taken the great step inward fully to centre themselves. This centring or grounding involves more than clearing oneself in relation to others of a consensus-culture-reality. It also involves a rediscovery of the animal within us and of our vital kinship with nature.

Culture via socialization and acculturation of the child fills the void, the schism in human nature between the animal in us and that godlike awareness alluded to earlier. Latent in all of us, this awareness occasionally bursts through in moments of creative insight or transcendent ecstasy. Similarly, our animal feelings of anger, pain, and joy may burst through and suddenly swamp our rational computer-consciousness. In both these states of consciousness we momentarily "lose control," and the computer part of our nervous systems cannot respectively describe the ineffable or control the beast. Unfamiliar or socially unacceptable feelings may be disturbing, and the expression of animal emotions and irrational, mystical, and ineffable experiences may be ridiculed. The computer attempts to inhibit these two other states of waking consciousness because it has been programmed by others to conform to a culturally prescribed consensus reality. With total control of emotions and feelings, and of reflective and transcendent consciousness, the robot man endures.

Without culture man would not be man. But like atomic energy or antibiotics, culture can be destructive rather than a life-supporting and evolution-potentiating asset. Western society today holds much and does much for the individual, but at the same time we are destroying our environment, overconsuming, overpopulating, and facing an epidemic of people needing psychiatric help. These are the symptoms of disease, the forewarnings of death, of doomsday. They are not the growing pains of an evolving species, but the death throes of dinosaur social systems, and values and minds that are now maladapted and archaic. We must accept failure and learn from our errors—not hold on and try to keep them alive. Let them die without further suffering or destruction.

Once a man can get "unstuck" from the superego consensus reality of his culture, from his pseudoself, he has made the first step toward freedom and fulfillment of his life potential.

The next is to rediscover the animal within, to free it from the repressions and sublimations imposed by the computer-conscience of programmed conformity. To get in touch with feelings, with "gut reactions," is a major part of the Human Potential Movement. But this is only the beginning—next comes a relearning of how to relate to others. This "humanization" process can also broaden the perspectives so that one realizes again one's similarity to animals. Although they lack culture and higher reflective consciousness, many animals do have the same basic needs

American Indian artist Blackbear Bosin lucidly depicts the oneness of spirit and earth. Modern man gets lost in his earthly "doings" and
distractions and must rediscover his spirit and combine an ethic of reverence
for all life with commitment as well.

and feelings that we have. The realization of this—the continuum between man and beast—gives us a deeper feeling of oneness with our animal brothers. From this may stem a true sense of responsibility for the rights of others and for their conservation.

In countless ways our culture and mode of living remove us more and more from nature. The wilderness is replaced by a concrete forest of high-rise apartments and offices, and the flexible minds of the inhabitants are reprogrammed. Those raised in such environments wonder at their parents' desire to vacation in the country, where there is "nothing to do," unless they hopefully find a crowded drive-in campsite with showers, heated swimming pools, and power fixtures for their mobile apartments. In one generation the need for wilderness can be lost, as can the awareness that we are no less than animal and that our brothers of stream, forest, desert, and ocean have the same rights to live as we have.

This loss of contact with another reality—that of nature—combined with a deadening and repression of feelings and of the animal within us, is perhaps the most destructive force we have to counter. Loss of contact with this reality can allow a populace to destroy the earth in blind ignorance, dazzled by the energy-consuming and polluting artifacts of a dream-based technology.

To save the earth and the spirit of humanity does not entail a regressive return to nature as a counter-culture, antitechnology reaction. It involves, rather, an awakening of consciousness and a change in perception and values so that animal and plant and fellow man are seen for what they are (the thing in itself, for itself), rather than in terms of how we might utilize them. This shift in perception and cognition, giving equal rights to others rather than assigning values in terms of their utility, is a growth shift in awareness from an immature ego-bound dependency/manipulation to a more accepting and embracing state of being. In such a state of awareness people are valued not for what they do, but for who they are intrinsically. With a heightened awareness of each other blossoms respect for all life. A man will think twice before he manipulates or kills to fulfill his own needs. There may be no need to put a business rival down or to destroy a tree in order to accomplish certain goals. Alternative paths may be found—or other goals.

The way we see and relate to one another is reflected in the way we see and relate to nature. A tree is no more a thing or an object than a person, and with this change in awareness we will be less likely to destroy either, since they will not be seen as depersonalized objects.

Perception of oneself will also change, and a new vitality and sensuality will be felt and enjoyed.

This change in awareness would also show us our responsibility not only to ourselves but to others, both people and animals; in fact to all life forms. We would accept, without ego-involvement, our godlike responsibilities for our own destiny and for the future of every living creature on this earth. We would not abdicate our responsibility to some "god" or "others in power," but assume reponsibility for our own actions. Reflective consciousness, once awakened, would help us assess the possible consequences of our actions, too, and we would be no longer guilty of "blindness as we progress" and of progress by "trial and error."

Awareness of nature and a reawakening of our own animal nature is part of the new renaissance that will revitalize the dwindling wilderness and the human spirit alike. Once man can reestablish contact with his own animal nature and reaffirm his commitment to conserve nature, we may have hope for our children's children. Nature and animals can make us more fully human. And when man can also maintain contact with his higher consciousness, we may be confident of fulfilling whatever potential we wish to develop. Without the former, though, the latter would be simply unintegrated, ungrounded growth—balloon man, pie in the sky. But a higher consciousness emanating from a grounded and fully integrated being would simply be a man actualizing his potential. Feeling and awareness harmonized and flowing—the mind is in equipoise, the body alive and as sensuous as an animal. Two states of being and awareness alive and integrated: both animal and god.

Afterword

Between animal and man are many similarities. The animal in man shares similarities in basic brain structure, emotions, needs, and in communication, development, and socialization in infancy with other members of the animal kingdom. Greeting and other social rituals, social distance and personal space, and biorhythms and internal time are seen in both human and non-human animals alike.

Culture—values and perceptions—may separate man from animal and nature and also repress the animal within him. Basic needs and their expression and satisfaction, be they sexual, or for love and belonging, may be blocked or coerced and redirected by consensus values in the service of the "social machine." An abnormal state of dependency (other-directedness) in the society may facilitate indoctrination, conformity, and acceptance of needs and values that stunt individual growth and actualization of human potential. A society of anonymous worker ants evolves—faceless, depersonalized, and dehumanized. *Homo technos* surfaces, programmed like a robot with acquired needs and values. Mind and body are split, and performance, or "doing," takes precedence over feeling and "being."

Man was once a hunter and lived in harmony with nature. Can modern technological man regain this state of harmony or ecological equilibrium? His own salvation is in the conservation of wilderness and restoration of wildlife refuge and natural resources. A reverence for all life—animal, plant, and human alike—is desperately needed to free man's way of seeing and doing, of perceiving all around him in terms of how to use all to satisfy his needs and wants: The biosphere has become an ego-sphere of self-centred values. Knowledge is used to control and manipulate in order to support an extractive and exploitative "progressive" way of life. We need not halt progress, but rather alter it with a new set of priorities and values based on reverence for life and long-range humane goals rather than shortsighted planning in which crisis intervention (in the face of energy and population crises) are all too frequent.

Man without a body is a computer, a robot. With a body he has communication and communion with his animal self—and the potential to control body functions, diseases, and to "walk with the gods." Man without nature is sterile, cold, and mortal in the brief span of his own limited, transient world of artifacts and values. With nature he is at one with a greater whole, the living church where he communicates and has communion with others, both human and nonhuman. Philosophical and religious, ethno-centric and egocentric influences still pervade our thinking, attempting to convince us that man is created or is a creature apart from animals. The "beast" within us must be subdued. In truth the animal is beautiful and the monster is the blindness of our enculturated beliefs.

Kinship with all life must be expressed in *action* since belief alone is no longer enough. Above and beyond our own immediate needs we all have a responsibility as stewards of this small planet since we have a reflective consciousness unlike any other animal, so far as is known. With this consciousness we can control our own evolution and we must assume this responsibility fully, since we stepped out of the constraining laws of nature when we first domesticated plants and animals and developed a technology. Nature can no longer direct us—we must guide ourselves and cherish our heritage in all that is wild and natural.

By virtue of this consciousness there is a god within us; man *is* both animal and god. Man must integrate both these sides of his nature if he is to be truly human. Kinship with all life and responsibility would then be expressed above and beyond the self-limiting and often destructive motives and priorities of the culture. These would ultimately change through consensus. But the change must first come from within us. Faith alone is not enough. It must be expressed in action and motivated by a sense of commitment to others as well as to oneself. Mankind today faces a critical point in evolution. Irresponsibility will lead to continued destruction of the biosphere through overexploitation and overpopulation. Responsibility is commitment to life. Health is a state of equipoise, of harmony; and man's global schizophrenia can be healed. It is generated by the splitting of mind and body, where only a small part of the mind—the computer—is educated, while the animal and godlike levels of consciousness are denied expression, left to atrophy. It is also generated by man's ego, separating him from animals and nature, and by a culture that allows him to see the world and others only in terms of his egocentric needs. Unity of mind and body (man and his own nature), and of man with nature (technosphere and biosphere), will erase this schizophrenia and see us through this critical point in our evolution toward a unity of consciousness on a global scale, the seeds of which could take root in our minds today—a promise which we see at the interphase between animal and man.

Suggestions for Further Reading

Barlow, Wilfred. *The Alexander Technique.* New York, Knopf, 1973.

Dubos, Rene. *A God Within.* New York, Scribner's, 1972.

Fox, Michael W. *Concepts in Ethology.* Minneapolis, University of Minnesota Press, 1974.

Lowen, Alexander. *The Betrayal of the Body.* New York, Collier, 1967.

Maslow, Abraham H. *Toward a Psychology of Being.* New York, Van Nostrand Reinhold, 1968.

Rolf, Ida P. *Structural Integration.* San Francisco, Guild for Structural Integration, 1962.

Schutz, William C. *Here Comes Everybody.* New York, Harper & Row, 1971.

Schweitzer, Albert. *The Teaching of Reverence for Life.* New York, Holt, Rinehart and Winston, 1965.

Teilhard de Chardin, Pierre. *Man's Place in Nature.* New York, Harper & Row, 1966.